Those who see the "sweet" side of suffering are usually believers who have learned to lean hard on the grace of Jesus through every hurt and heartache. It's a good description for Esther Lovejoy as she opens her heart in *The Sweet Side of Suffering*. Congratulations, Esther, on compiling stirring insights from God's Word that will bless and inspire the reader.

Joni Eareckson Tada
Author and founder, Joni and Friends
International Disability Center

Esther Lovejoy wisely concludes that even in our deepest valleys, we may know the strength and intimacy that God affords us through the ministry of His precious Word. Her book is to be commended not only because it is born out of her work as a teacher and counselor but especially as a fellow traveler through the vale of tears and seasons of questions. There is a compassion, hope, and encouragement in these pages for the reader.

Ravi Zacharias
Author and speaker

Esther's experience of suffering not only takes you *to* Calvary, it takes you *through* Calvary into the closest communion with Christ, our Wounded Healer. Her testimony of personal suffering gives liberty for those in pain to allow their grief to carry them into the presence of the Lord and to experience Him in the deepest way.

Dominic Herbst, M.S., M.A.
Therapist, consultant, and public speaker
Founder and president, Bethesda Family Services Foundation
Author, *Restoring Relationships*

Engaging and inspiring, this book provides hope for those who otherwise are hopeless. The author, who herself has experienced much disappointment and pain, has a wonderful narrative style that allows her to communicate what can be gained by a biblically informed understanding of suffering in a deeply insightful yet practical way. Read this book. It is time and effort well spent. Your experience of suffering will not be the same.

Peter C. Hill, Ph.D.
Professor and Undergraduate Chair,
Rosemead School of Psychology, Biola University
Editor, *Journal of Psychology and Christianity*
Co-Editor, *Baker Encyclopedia of Psychology and Counseling*

Esther Lovejoy speaks from the crucible of her own deep experiences. She has suffered, and she found what she calls "the sweet side of suffering" when she fellowshipped with the Savior in the Garden alone. Her message in this book is a helpful one for all of us who find ourselves in the midst of the dark places.

Dr. Thomas P. Bailey
Professor emeritus and past president,
Nyack College and Alliance Theological Seminary

# the sweet side of suffering

## RECOGNIZING GOD'S BEST WHEN FACING LIFE'S WORST

M. Esther Lovejoy

DISCOVERY HOUSE

PUBLISHERS®

*Feeding the Soul with the Word of God*

Discovery House is affiliated with RBC Ministries,
Grand Rapids, Michigan.

Requests for permission to quote from this book should be directed to:
Permissions Department, Discovery House Publishers, P.O. Box 3566,
Grand Rapids, MI 49501, or contact us by e-mail at
permissionsdept@dhp.org

**Library of Congress Cataloging-in-Publication Data**

Lovejoy, M. Esther.
 The sweet side of suffering : recognizing God's best when facing life's
worst / M. Esther Lovejoy.
    pages cm
 Includes bibliographical references and index.
 ISBN 978-1-57293-745-1
 1.  Consolation. 2.  Suffering--Religious aspects--Christianity.  I. Title.
 BV4905.3.L685 2013
 248.8'6--dc23
                                                          2012047494

Printed in the United States of America
Second printing in 2013

*To my mother, Mary McGarvey,*
*who laid a solid foundation from which I could learn these truths,*
*and continues to sweetly display all that she has taught.*

# Contents

# Acknowledgments

FOR ME IT BEGAN at the age of eight at a little red table decorated with nursery rhyme decals. I placed a blank piece of paper on the table, thoughtfully picked up a #2 pencil, and began my first book. It bore the lofty title *When Revival Comes*, inspired by a passion for revival that was my father's and a passion for writing that was my own. The "book" was never finished, and its few pages are long gone, but the dream of that eight-year-old girl has remained.

A. W. Tozer said, "The only book that should ever be written is one that flows up from the heart . . . You should never write a book unless you just have to." Over the years I've thought of many things I could write about, but nothing had to be written—until now. The deep desire to express what I've learned through suffering has finally met Tozer's qualifications.

God has used many people to bring about the fulfillment of a young girl's dream, and I want to express my sincere thanks for their encouragement and help along the way.

Dave Fessenden—you have been a friend, an encourager, and a light along a new and unfamiliar path. Thanks for your guidance.

Marlene Bagnull—God has used you to open doors in an industry where it's often hard to even find the knob. Thank you for being sensitive to our Father's voice.

Cec Murphey—thank you for your willingness to invest in the dreams of others.

Becky English—thank you for believing in the message of this book and offering practical help and suggestions.

Diana Flegal—thank you for being my agent, cheerleader, and friend.

Judy Markham—thank you for your touch on these words that brought clarity to this important message. You have been wise and gentle—the perfect combination for an editor.

And a thank you that can't be fully expressed to my wonderful (and patient) husband who has lovingly nagged this book into existence. Thank you for believing that dreams can come true.

*"Know for certain that your descendants will be strangers in a country not their own, and they will be enslaved and mistreated four hundred years . . . and afterwards they will come out with great possessions."*

GENESIS 15:13—14

# Introduction

*"I will give you the treasures of darkness,*
*riches stored in secret places,*
*so that you may know that I am the L*ORD,
*the God of Israel, who summons you by name."*

ISAIAH 45:3

IN THE SIXTIES, a popular folk song by Joni Mitchell expressed the idea that even after looking at love from both sides, it was still the illusions of love that were remembered. I've looked at suffering from both sides now, and it leaves no illusions. Suffering is a reality that demands our full attention. Whether in the midst of suffering, or looking back on it, you are left with no false impressions about the pain and heartache that encompass it. But suffering offers something else—something that is equally real. It offers a wonderfully surprising sweet side.

I have shared the sufferings of many people in my years of ministry, and now, in more recent years, I have experienced suffering firsthand. And while I know suffering from "both sides now," I also know its unexpected joys, its value and worth, the treasures that are found only in the dark places. Most of all, I know, in a deeper and more personal way, the Man of Sorrows who has walked with me every step.

Max Lucado declares, "A season of suffering is a small price to pay for a close view of God."[1] This doesn't minimize the suffering, but points out the value of all that we gain in return.

For most of us, suffering is not a choice. It is forced on us; it rudely interrupts our lives and demands our full attention. Given the choice, we would not welcome suffering into our lives in any form, but we're usually not given that choice. We are, however, given another choice and that is the choice of how we respond to this intruder.

It's important to understand from the very onset of this book that the sweet side of suffering is not automatically granted to everyone who suffers. We have all seen the bitterness and anger that suffering can produce. We have known those who have never recovered from the onslaught of its pain and heartache, or those who have chosen a permanent escape rather than face the hopelessness they've felt in their personal suffering. For these, a sweet side never existed. In fact, for many, the thought that suffering could have even an element of sweetness is a laughable, foolish, unattainable myth.

It's also important to understand that while the sweet side of suffering is not immediately apparent, it can be found. It's the "treasures of darkness" recorded by David in the psalms— treasures that have to be sought. It's the "gold by moonlight"[2] experienced by Amy Carmichael—gold that must be mined. The sweet side of suffering *can* be found, and I would go further and say that to come out of any experience of suffering whole, it *must* be found.

A beautiful illustration of this principle is found in the

story of the nation of Israel and their exodus from Egypt—the land of their suffering. God must have appeared indifferent, or even heartless, to these slaves as the promise of freedom was snatched from them time after time. But God's timing was perfect, and when they left they took with them the plunder of Egypt (Exodus 12:36). The very source of their suffering became the source of great riches. And so it can be for us.

Paul says to the Galatians, "Have you suffered so much for nothing?" (Galatians 3:4). For our purposes, Paul could be asking, "Have you suffered so much without experiencing the sweet side?" What a sad commentary on someone's experience of suffering—to have gone through it for nothing. And yet I have found that to be the experience of many people.

Why waste suffering? When it forces its way into our lives, when it intrudes upon our orderly world unbidden, why not squeeze out of it every good thing, every ounce of value that it can possibly offer. Why not use it rather than be its victim? The only difference between meaningless suffering and the value of suffering is into whose hand we place it.

Years ago I drew a primitive picture to illustrate this thought. In the first scene, suffering is placed in the hands of our enemy, Satan, and becomes a tool of destruction. You see him hammering away, using it to destroy and shatter his victim. In the second scene, suffering is placed in the hands of our loving Savior who wields it only to create function and great beauty. Same tool. Often the same pain. But far different results. Satan's only objective is our total defeat. God's concern is always for the greater good—our best and His glory. Satan's hands are prompted by a heart of pure evil and hatred. God's hands are inspired by unfailing love and goodness. Both can hurt, but only one has a sweet side.

The intention of this book is not to delve into an explanation for suffering, or to be a forum for debating the "whys" of pain. Furthermore, it is not my purpose to defend or explain God. Nor is this an effort to get you to "put on a happy face," to look on the bright side, or to develop a Pollyanna attitude. Instead, it is my prayer that my words and my experience will be an encouragement for those who are suffering. I want to cheer you on, to pull you out of the awful heaviness of despair and give you hope. I want to point you to the One who can bring hope and healing, comfort and guidance through the murky, dreadful mire of suffering.

I want you to not just read about the sweet side of suffering, but to personally find and experience it. That can only come through the hands that have scars as an eternal reminder of how He suffered for us. The One who brings sweetness has experienced the full extent of human suffering—and He *did* have a choice!

Another important thing to note is that suffering is still suffering. There is still pain and heartache involved. There are still unanswered questions and struggles with very human emotions.

I remember, some years ago, coming upon a group of women talking in glowing terms to a younger woman about to have her first baby. They were far enough removed from their own experiences of childbirth that they spoke of it in sentimental terms. It was "the most wonderful experience a woman could have," "such fulfillment," "the greatest joy." And on and on they went. Having gone through the experience of labor and delivery fairly recently, I added this little tidbit of reality as I walked by: "And it will hurt!"

Later the new mother shared with me how thankful she

was that I had added those words. She said that she was feeling so defeated during childbirth because there was a lot of pain and not a lot of euphoria. Then she remembered my words, "And it will hurt!" She was grateful for that reminder.

I don't want to be guilty of making the same mistake as I talk about suffering that those women did as they spoke in such glowing terms about childbirth. While I share the wonders of the hidden joys that can be found during suffering, I don't want to ignore the fact that it is still suffering. So let me say it again, "And it will hurt!" It is the fact that there can be true sweetness in the midst of some of our deepest human pain that is so amazing. It may hurt so bad. But the good news is that it can also hurt so good.

My oldest daughter was born with a minor problem with her left leg. It was slightly twisted. While there was no immediate risk, there was the potential for more serious problems later in her life. The doctor offered us two possible solutions. One was to wait a few months and have her fitted for a brace that would gradually (and painfully) pull that leg into line. The other was to take advantage of the softness and flexibility of her newborn bones and work immediately to straighten them. He strongly recommended the latter. We trusted his judgment and agreed to do whatever was necessary to straighten that little leg.

The decision was easy; the reality of what that involved was much harder. A couple of times each day I had to take Debbie's little foot and gently turn it. The only way I knew that I had turned it enough was when she cried.

I had waited a lifetime (or so it seemed) to be a mother. I had wanted babies from the time I wasn't one. My husband and I were married almost six long and worrisome years before Debbie, our first child, finally arrived. And now I was to take this precious baby and twist her foot twice a day until it hurt enough for her to cry out.

How could I possibly do such a thing to my child? How could I intentionally inflict pain on one I loved so much? I'll tell you how. I could do it for the simple reason that I knew it was for her best; I knew that it would spare her more pain and suffering in later years.

And so twice a day I took that adorable little foot in my hand—a hand that at all other times was gentle and tender—and twisted until she cried. Until we both cried. My only motive was love. My only concern was her best. I would look down at that precious little girl and know that she couldn't possibly understand what was in my heart. She only felt what came from my hands.

The parallels are obvious. God loves us. There aren't words to convey the depths of His love, although there is a cross that gives us a glimpse of its depths. My love for Debbie pales in comparison. Yet I was willing, for her sake, to do what she could not possibly understand; in fact, what she could easily misunderstand or mistake for cruelty.

"For I know the plans I have for you," declared the Lord to His people, "plans to prosper you and not to harm you, plans to give you hope *a*nd a future" (Jeremiah 29:11). And sometimes He has to twist our foot to accomplish what He knows is best.

I LOVE TO TALK about God, and I can't wait to share Him with you through these pages. I love to talk about His faithfulness and love during my own suffering, but that brings with it a dilemma. How much of my story should I share? I need you to know that I am not writing from a vacuum or just expressing theory. I need to share with you some of my own pain and heartache so that it can be the backdrop against which you can best see God's goodness and mercy.

Often suffering catches us by surprise. It was that way for me. My husband, who was a pastor, arrived to pick me up as usual one day, and when I got in the car, he turned to me and said, "We're leaving the ministry." I was stunned! Ministry was our calling and our lives. But what came next was even more stunning. I learned that he had been living a hidden life of sin that spanned the entire thirty years of our marriage. His involvement in various sinful activities was serious enough that he was not only removed from ministry, but eventually stripped of his ordination. Sadly, it also destroyed our marriage.

Those are the facts most simply stated. But the reality of those facts left me with an overwhelming sense of betrayal and a depth of emotional pain that cannot be expressed in words. However, it was also during those difficult days that I felt as never before the presence and unfailing love of my Savior and learned many important lessons about the sweet side of suffering.

God, in His infinite goodness, brought "beauty from ashes" as I later married my high school sweetheart. Peter and I have a tremendous marriage that is wonderfully summed up by my new last name—Lovejoy! However, we too have faced some times of deep suffering and the lessons have continued.

In the years of our marriage we have struggled to keep a business afloat, resulting in years of financial hardship.

Eventually, we lost our business and, subsequently, our home. I have fought discouragement, despair, fear, and even depression, and you will hear the echo of those in these pages. And yet these years have also brought a new depth of understanding of the reality of that sweetness that is unique to suffering. Would I want to live a minute of those years over again? Absolutely not! But neither do I regret those years of struggles as God revealed himself to us in new and deeper ways.

There are also other instances of suffering too personal too share, but suffering is not unique to me. Many others have suffered—many in worse ways than I have experienced. But the joy celebrated in this book is that the sweet side of suffering is also not unique to me. It is there because of God alone, and it is offered to all of His children who find themselves "in the midst."

When the author Robert Louis Stevenson was a small child, he was staring out the window of his home on a dark night watching the lamplighter work his way down the street. When his mother asked Robert what he was doing, he replied, "I'm watching that man poke holes in the darkness."

Times of suffering can be times of tremendous darkness of soul. It is my prayer that these pages will help poke holes in the darkness and bring God's light and encouragement to those who are in the midst of the dark night of suffering.

## CHAPTER 1

# The Sweetness of His Voice

*And He walks with me, and He talks with me.*
CHARLES AUSTIN MILES, "IN THE GARDEN"

MORNING CHAPEL WAS REQUIRED at the college I attended, and most students went out of duty rather than desire. Often the services were dry and boring, and we used that time to cram for tests or catch up on reading. However, I recall one chapel service when a professor took advantage of his pulpit time to mock the hymn "In the Garden." He did a thorough job and we, in our immaturity, found it immensely amusing.

But I remember at the same time feeling slightly uncomfortable. I thought back to church services where older people had requested that hymn and then had sung it with a look of rapture on their faces. Had they experienced something real that my professor was so lightly and cleverly writing off as flights of fancy?

I also wondered about the hymn writer. What had led

him to so poetically express such an intimacy with God? Was it truly possible to have God walk with me and talk with me? Could I hear Him assure me personally that I was His own? Could I too experience the shared joy that comes from lingering with the divine? While the language was flowery, the experience was wonderfully real for this hymn writer and many others. And I wanted it.

Many years have passed since that college chapel service. Since then, I have walked with Him and talked with Him, and some of our sweetest conversations have taken place as He's walked with me through times of suffering.

I will never forget the night following my husband's disclosure of his hidden life of sin. I couldn't sleep. I couldn't think. I couldn't pray. I could only hurt. And so I sat. Just sat. And the Lord sat with me. All night He sat with me. It was, in retrospect, one of my most intimate times with the Lord. I didn't talk and He didn't talk. He just stayed with me. But as night faded into a new day—a day that I didn't want to face—the Lord began to quietly speak to me.

"He speaks, and the sound of His voice is so sweet. . . ." My college professor found those words amusing. I found them a lifeline. God's voice was sweet, but it was also practical. He gently gave me insight that I needed, strength that I didn't have, and a boldness that this new situation required. His words were truly "an ever-present help in trouble" (Psalm 46:1).

### LEARNING TO KNOW HIS VOICE

But how did I know it was God's voice? How could I distinguish His voice from my own thoughts and ideas? Jesus reminds us in John 10:3 that the sheep know the voice of their shepherd. I knew His voice. I knew it because it was a voice I had heard many times before. I had developed a listening ear over the years and the sound of His voice was familiar to me. But that had not always been the case.

Growing up I had always struggled with "devotions." I had been raised in the church, and since I was a child I had heard about the importance of daily Bible reading and prayer. I knew it was important; I just didn't seem to be able to do it—except for the first few days of January and for a week or two after summer youth camp. In spite of that, I seemed to be doing just fine. I loved the Lord. I wasn't rebellious. I was a good kid. So why the big fuss about daily devotions?

Then came marriage, small children, and the demands of full-time ministry. How could I possibly be expected to have meaningful quiet time with three small children and a phone that rang nonstop? No time for garden walks with the Lord. Besides, I was doing great. I loved being a pastor's wife, I loved being a mother, and I still loved the Lord.

What I didn't realize was that the only righteousness that can grow apart from regular walks with the Gardener is self-righteousness—and I had that in abundance. Don't get me wrong. I did read my Bible: I read it to prepare for Sunday school lessons. I read it to find great truths and exciting insights for Bible studies. I read it to prepare notes for speaking and teaching. I read it to give out. I talked it, but I didn't listen to it.

Then, one day, I came to an important realization. If I was going to tell people that this book, this Bible, contained all the wisdom needed for life, all the answers to life's problems, then I had better begin to find them there for my own life. And thus began a discipline that has continued for many years. I determined that whatever I faced, I would expect God to give me an answer from His Word.

I began by purchasing a small spiral notebook. In the front I would write down the verse that I felt God had "spoken" to me during my quiet time with Him and then a brief written prayer in response. In the back I would write down any problem that I faced—big or small. Then I would write the word "Scripture" and ask God to give me a specific answer or guidance from His Word. He has *never* failed to do that.

He has not always given me the answer I wanted. Sometimes, because of His great mercy, He has not given me the answer I deserved. But He has always given an answer. Today, my pile of notebooks is quite large and spans many years.

God speaks, and over the years I have established a discipline of listening that has sustained me in the difficult and dark days.

## HEARING HIM IN HIS WORD

He speaks! He truly speaks, and He speaks most clearly and simply through His Word. The psalmist says, "If your law had not been my delight, I would have perished in my affliction" (Psalm 119:92). There was a time when I thought that the psalmist was over-reacting, or perhaps being a little melodramatic. Now I know better. I echo that heartfelt and intense declaration and can honestly say that if it weren't for the ministry of God's Word to me during some of life's toughest times, I don't know how I would have made it. Truly!

However, I suspect that the psalmist didn't wait until his time of affliction to delight in God's law. The sheep learn to know the shepherd's voice in the ordinary days of life so that in a time of crisis it can be immediately recognized. It is so much easier to hear God speak to us in our affliction and suffering if we have established a habit of listening to His words, of recognizing and responding to His voice during the easier times of life.

Hearing His voice begins with learning to read His Word with a listening ear. There is a huge difference between reading God's Word and hearing God's voice. You can read chapter after chapter and never hear Him speak. Or you can read just a word or a phrase and know that He has spoken those words to you. They have become personal and current—speaking specifically to your need and your circumstances. Sometimes it's words of guidance that you hear. Sometimes it's encouragement. There are times when you hear Him utter sweet words of comfort, and then there are times when His voice lovingly corrects or rebukes. His Word becomes His words—personal and clear.

My journals stand as wonderful evidence of this truth. As I journey back through the years, I am amazed again at how specific and practical God's Word is to my real situations and needs. I have been awed by God's answers, by His counsel, by His love and encouragement, and by His promises. He has never failed to speak. But these answers came because I listened. I came to Him, asked Him to speak, and then waited to hear what He would say.

## "But There Is a God in Heaven"

One such time was when I was facing a situation that seemed utterly hopeless. I wanted a baby—desperately wanted a baby! My heart ached to be a mother, but year after year passed, and my hope diminished with each passing year. Hopelessness is probably one of the most devastating and crippling of all human emotions and yet is an emotion often associated with suffering. We truly do face some situations for which there are no apparent answers and hope seems gone.

It was at this point in my life that God gave me words that have sustained me time and time again, words that I have shared to encourage many others in similar situations.

These words are found in the book of Daniel, and the backdrop for them is also a hopeless situation. King Nebuchadnezzar of Babylon had a dream and, as was typical of that day and age, he called for his wise men and magicians to determine the meaning of his dream. There was just one hitch. He either couldn't remember the dream or chose not to share it. And so the dream experts were given this assignment: tell the king his dream and what it means or die!

How's that for motivation? But even with their lives in the balance they were unable to fulfill the king's command and desperately tried to explain that no man (or magician) on earth could do what he had requested.

However, kings expect to be obeyed, and so the edict went out that all the wise men in the kingdom were to be killed. When this word reached Daniel, a young Hebrew in captivity in Babylon, he asked the reason for this extreme measure by the king. He was informed of the apparently hopeless situation and the king's frustration with the failure of his interpreters to produce the desired results.

Daniel's response was simple. First he went to prayer, and then he went to the king—in that order. He waited to hear the voice of the King of Kings before speaking to the Babylonian king.

Daniel's initial approach to Nebuchadnezzar was very much like that of the other wise men and magicians: He declared that what the king had asked was impossible. No man could do this! And then Daniel added these seven wonderful words: "But there is a God in heaven" (Daniel 2:28).

I love these words. I love both the simplicity and the wonderful profoundness of these words. They give hope to a hopeless situation. What was impossible becomes Him-possible. "But there is a God in heaven," and He can alter human circumstances. This God can give grace, He can heal, He can forgive, He can move mountains. He can accomplish whatever is best and right and good. And Daniel's confidence was that He could even reveal unknown dreams and their meanings.

What we face may truly be impossible humanly. There may be no apparent answer or solution. The situation may seem utterly and frighteningly hopeless. "But there is a God in heaven"—and that truth is enough.

It was enough for Daniel, and it was enough for me. My circumstances didn't change, but my heart did. I rested in those wonderful words and knew that what couldn't be changed by man could be changed by God. There was hope because there was God—a God who was all-seeing, all-knowing, all-powerful, all-wise, and all-loving.

### HEARING HIS PROMISE

God did bless us with children, and it was one of those "blessings" that brought us to another time of great heartache and suffering—a suffering that has been shared by many Christian parents.

My oldest daughter, Debbie, decided to go her own way and became involved in a lifestyle that caused me much fear. As a pastor's wife I had wept with many mothers whose children had chosen to walk away from the Lord. Now their pain was mine.

One of the wonderful things about our heavenly Father is that He often prepares us for a difficult time. Months before I was aware of my own child's struggles, I had found a wonderful book by Peter Lord entitled *Keeping the Doors Open.*[1] In it he shares his own experiences as a father of rebellious children (not just "child," but "children"!). I found it a very encouraging and practical book that I intended to use in counseling and praying with others—a textbook.

Little did I realize that God was preparing my own heart. While there was much in Peter Lord's book that was helpful, one thing stood out as God's clear voice to me. In the book, Pastor Lord shared his wife's response to their heartache. She got alone with the Lord and determined to stay there until she had a specific promise from Him regarding her child.

I determined to do the same thing for Debbie. I spent time in prayer and in the Scriptures, and the day came when God, through His Word, gave me His promise for my wayward child. His promise offered assurance and hope that contradicted everything I was seeing lived out before me as I watched the deliberate steps of my own child away from God's best. It was God's Word to which I clung over and over again in the months that followed. And it is God's promise that I have seen beautifully fulfilled in her life.

What did God say? What was His promise to me for my daughter? It was these words from Ezekiel that became my basis for hope:

> "This is what the Sovereign LORD says: On the day I cleanse you from all your sins, I will resettle your towns, and the ruins will be rebuilt. The desolate land will be cultivated instead of lying desolate in the sight of all

who pass through it. They will say, 'This land that was laid waste has become like the garden of Eden . . . Then the nations around you that remain will know that I the LORD have rebuilt what was destroyed and have replanted what was desolate. I the LORD have spoken, and I will do it" (Ezekiel 36:33–36).

These verses begin with the wonderful assurance that it is God who is speaking: "This is what the Sovereign Lord says." I needed to know that these words came to me from One who was able to fulfill them. It was so important to remember who was speaking because the impact of these words was directly related to the authority of the speaker.

When Satan would taunt me with doubts and question my hope for Debbie's restoration, my best defense was to yell back, "God says!" It reminded me of when my children were little and I would send the youngest child out to call the others in for dinner. His older siblings didn't respond to a command issued by their younger brother until he added, "Mom says!" Those words added authority to his little voice, just as God's words gave authority to mine.

And look at how these verses end. Once again God gives assurance that these words are from Him and that they carry His guarantee as He declares, "I the LORD have spoken, and I will do it." What hope that gave me!

I learned something during this time about our Enemy. He is a skilled artist and can draw vivid and horrible pictures in our minds about the future. They are always pictures of our worst fears—pictures that don't include God's promises or His grace. And they are pictures that seem all too possible.

Many, many times (usually at night) I had to purposely

look away from what I was seeing in Debbie and from the picture the Enemy was painting of her future. In a determined, deliberate way I had to choose instead to look to the promise God had given me for my child.

God's words to me were encouraging, but I didn't realize until much later how specific they were to Debbie's needs. There was much of her that had been destroyed—much that was in ruins and "lying desolate." The months that followed revealed the reality and extent of this, and I realized more and more the need for God to do exactly what He had promised in His Word.

And He did! "I the Lord have spoken, and I will do it." This was a work that could only be done by God. He used many instruments and, like all renovation, it took much time—but He did what He had promised.

I have to say in all honesty that I don't know how I would have made it through the painful process of Debbie's restoration without having heard God's voice so clearly and so specifically. It helped to know how it would all end.

Today, this same girl is restored and "rebuilt"—a mother and pastor's wife ministering in the Haitian community of Miami. In particular, she is trying to love to Jesus some challenging and needy teens.

How very different the reality is from the picture that the Enemy had so vividly painted for me of Debbie's future. Her life is a fulfillment of the promise God gave to me in my time of fear. He speaks, and the sound of His voice is not only so sweet, but so trustworthy.

## LISTENING WITH EXPECTATION

Listening for God's voice is something that we also see modeled throughout Scripture. Habakkuk is a wonderful example of someone who heard God's voice in his time of suffering.

Habakkuk was annoyed at the injustice he saw all around him, and frustrated with God's apparent lack of concern. The book of Habakkuk begins with the prophet expressing some of these complaints and then waiting to hear how God would respond. He says, "I will look to see what he will say to me" (Habakkuk 2:1).

What a tremendous example. Habakkuk didn't allow suffering to drive him away from God, but came to God in complete honesty, expecting a response. And God answered. The book of Habakkuk ends with a complete change of attitude on the prophet's part. His complaining turned to rejoicing, not because of a change in his circumstances, but because he had heard from God.

When we are facing times of confusion in our suffering, when we are confused by God's ways, our human nature often tends to withdraw from God. Instead, God invites us to come to Him as Habakkuk did, to honestly vent our complaints and then "look to see what he will say." It is His voice alone that can turn complaining to rejoicing.

The circumstances in my own life have not always caused me to rejoice. In fact, they have often been the source of much grief. However, I believe that joy can be found *in the midst* of the grief, not just in the absence of grief, and the source of much of that joy is found in our Savior's voice.

We have a God who has always initiated communication. He wants to talk to us. His first contact with Adam and Eve was to walk and talk with them in the garden. Sin broke the sweetness of that fellowship, but God continues to seek for ways to communicate with His children. We can still "come to the garden alone" and find Him ready to walk with us and talk with us because, after all, we truly are His own.

I have never been more fully aware of God's presence and His voice than during some of my times of bitterest sorrow and suffering. The psalmist assures us that "the LORD is close to the brokenhearted" (Psalm 34:18). He draws near so that He can communicate His comfort and His love, so that He can give guidance and encouragement. He draws near so that we can more easily hear His voice as He pours His love into us in our time of need.

One of the sweetest things in the midst of our darkest hours is the sound of our Savior's voice.

*And He walks with me, and He talks with me,*
*And He tells me I am His own.*
*And the joy we share as we tarry there,*
*None other has ever known.*[2]

## CHAPTER 2

# The Sweetness of Knowing God

*"I will give them a heart to know me, that I am the LORD."*
JEREMIAH 24:7

"HOW COME THERE are so many more stars in Africa than at home?" That was my question to a friend I was visiting in Burkina Faso a number of years ago. I had never seen an abundance of stars like I saw that night. The black sky was full of pinpoints of light in an amazing display.

Her answer was simple as she explained that I had never before been where it was so dark. Where I live, there are so many other lights that compete with the light of the stars that many of them are not visible. In the absolute darkness of an African night, with no nearby city lights to diminish the darkness, the stars shine unhindered.

I have thought of that often since then when I have found myself in the dark times of my life—when I have been where it was so dark. And it was against that dark backdrop that I was able to see more details of God's character and nature than ever before.

In the brightness of good times we often miss some of the most wonderful and intimate details of God, but against the blackness of suffering we see pinpoints of light that we never noticed before. And they are beautiful to behold. The great preacher Charles Spurgeon said, "God's people have always found out the best of their God when in the worst of conditions."[1]

Job is a perfect illustration of this. Job's name is synonymous with suffering, and his story can hardly be equaled. Yet after all he endured, Job was able to declare: "My ears had heard of you but now my eyes have seen you" (Job 42:5). Now, in the midst of this suffering—against the backdrop of this very black sky—my eyes have seen you, Lord. Now I don't just know about you, I know *you*! Through suffering, God shattered Job's theology to allow Job to see His reality.

That can be our experience too. To quote Max Lucado again, "A season of suffering is a small price to pay for a close view of God."[2] I would add that a season of suffering seems to afford us that close view, often better than the seasons of ease when other "lights" can interfere.

Think of the many women and men of faith who have inspired us. Think of Amy Carmichael, Dietrich Bonhoeffer, and Jim Elliot. Think of Corrie ten Boom and Joni Eareckson Tada. What is it about their lives that has allowed us to see God so clearly?

It's more than just the drama of their particular stories—more than their suffering. I believe it is that we see God in their suffering; we catch a glimpse of the reality and presence of a loving heavenly Father that shines forth in the midst of their circumstances. And I am convinced that if we will look past the pain of what we're experiencing, we can see God in our own story of suffering as well.

We are often encouraged in Scripture to "magnify the Lord." I have thought a lot recently about what that word means. In its most practical use, *magnify* means to view something, usually through a lens, in a way that allows us to see it more clearly and in greater detail.

Our suffering is that lens. It offers us a magnified view of God, a view in which we are able to see Him more clearly and in much greater detail. And what we find are details about God that perfectly meet our needs.

### THE SOURCE OF ALL WE NEED

Peter begins his second letter with these words: "Grace and peace be yours in abundance" (2 Peter 1:2). How desperately we need both grace and peace during our times of suffering. But what is their source? Where can we find grace and peace in abundance? Peter goes on to give us the answer. They are available "through the *knowledge* of God and of Jesus our Lord. His divine power has given us everything we need for life and godliness *through our knowledge of him*" (2 Peter 1:2–3, italics added).

I love the absolutes of Scripture: all, none, never, everything, always. In these words, Peter makes an amazing claim: God's divine power has made available to us *everything* we need to live this life—and to live it as godly men and women. Everything! But it is important to remember the source. It is our knowledge of God that offers us this unlimited supply.

One of the lessons that I've learned as I've gotten to know God through my own times of struggle is that sometimes He will withhold what *we think* we must have for life in order to give us what *He knows* we must have for godliness. It is not always a comfortable exchange, but it is always a worthwhile one.

When Peter and I were first married, he earnestly prayed that we would learn to know God better. In the years that followed, some of our prayers regarding our business seemed to go unanswered. I didn't immediately understand that what seemed to be God's lack of response to those urgent prayers was actually part of His answer to the greater prayer—that we learn to know Him better. He will sometimes sacrifice what seems good for what is best.

His answer was not one we would have chosen. In recent years we've lost much, including our business and our home—things that we thought we had to have for life. But in exchange God has given us what *He* knew we needed for godliness. In these times of loss, we have gained a new and deeper knowledge of God. We have gained far more than we have lost!

Paul, who was no novice at suffering, puts it like this: "I consider everything a loss compared to the surpassing greatness of knowing Christ Jesus my Lord, for whose sake I have lost all things. I consider them rubbish, that I may gain Christ" (Philippians 3:8).

The NIV actually cleans up Paul's vocabulary a little, and in doing so we lose some of the impact. Paul actually says that all that he has lost is "dung" or manure in comparison to the "surpassing greatness" of knowing Christ. How amazing that suffering offers us this unique opportunity to get to know the eternal God of the universe; and in getting to know God, we find what we need to endure and even triumph through our suffering. He offers grace and peace in abundance and all that we need for life and godliness *through* our knowledge of Him.

## Great Is His Faithfulness

What are some specific aspects of God's character that we learn to know through suffering? A couple stand out to me as the "brightest stars" of the night.

Peter and I chose the hymn "Great Is Thy Faithfulness" to be sung at our wedding. We chose it as a testimony to God's faithfulness in our individual lives that had brought us to this amazing moment. It was our song of triumph—or so we thought. Little did we realize that it would become the theme of the first years of our marriage as we faced unbelievably trying and difficult circumstances.

I had read Jeremiah's declaration of God's faithfulness in Lamentations 3:23 many times before, but had never really focused on the context of his words. Was the prophet having one of those great days and just couldn't help but break into praise for God's great faithfulness? It seems logical to think that he made this statement when the faithfulness of God was especially evident and when life was daily proof of the goodness and faithfulness of a loving heavenly Father. But that was not the case at all, and Jeremiah's surroundings at the time that he declared this truth about his God gave little evidence of God's great faithfulness. Instead, Jeremiah was in the midst of deep personal and national suffering.

For me, Jeremiah's circumstances add strength to his words. These are not the words of a man coming up with a nice saying for a future hymn writer to put to music. They are not words meant to be an easy Christian slogan to be hung on our walls or embroidered on our pillows. These words were the heart cry of a man in the worst of surroundings who was declaring what he knew to be true about his God, even in the midst of the darkness of his circumstances.

As I look back over these past years that have included so much personal suffering, I think the star that shines the brightest against my dark sky is God's faithfulness. He has been faithful in all circumstances to provide, to guide, to protect, to comfort, to correct. Great has been His faithfulness!

I have always known that God is faithful. He was certainly faithful throughout all my years that were free of suffering. But His faithfulness was one of those stars that blended into the brightness of my life so that I hardly noticed it. But then it got dark, and that darkness gave me a clear glimpse of His faithfulness that has been a lifeline for me over and over again.

This was also the testimony of the psalmist. In Psalm 89:8 he exclaims, "O LORD God Almighty, who is like you? You are mighty, O LORD, and your faithfulness surrounds you." This same thought is expressed in a favorite verse of mine found in Isaiah 11:5 where the writer gives us a wonderful picture of God's faithfulness surrounding him when he says, "Righteousness will be his belt and faithfulness the sash around his waist."

What made this verse especially meaningful to me was my own experience with a sash. I had three children of preschool age at the same time, which made every shopping trip an adventure. In fact, if food hadn't been a necessity, I might have given up grocery shopping altogether! How do you manage two toddlers and an infant who still needs to be carried—especially in a busy parking lot? My solution was my coat. I purposely bought a coat that had a sash around the waist. Debbie and Danny had strict instructions that they were each to hold on to an end of that sash (with threat of dire consequences if they let go) while I carried Steven. My children knew that I followed through with "dire consequences," so they obeyed and were safe.

It was when walking through a frightening time that I first discovered the assurance that I could cling to His faithfulness and be safe. At the time, we were counseling a young woman who was a prostitute and a drug dealer with mob connections. We made a number of people very unhappy as Linda's lifestyle began to change. They were unhappy enough to make some serious threats against our family. This was way out of my comfort zone. In fact, this was downright scary. So I cried out to the Lord and the verse He gave me was Isaiah 11:5: "Righteousness will be his belt and faithfulness the sash around his waist." Instantly, to my mind came the image of my children hanging on to my sash. I was now the child, and I was walking through a dangerous and scary place. But I held on tightly to God's faithfulness and, just as my sash had kept my children safe, His sash of faithfulness kept me safe.

We learned later that God had miraculously intervened one night when there were plans to harm us. Great is His faithfulness!

## A LOVE THAT WILL NOT FAIL

Jeremiah, in his time of deep distress, also points us to another star that shone brightly against his dark sky of suffering. In Lamentations 3:21–22 he declares, "Yet this I call to mind and therefore I have hope: Because of the LORD's great love we are not consumed, for his compassions never fail." Jeremiah placed his hope in the truth of God's unfailing love.

I love the fact that in Scripture those two words, *unfailing* and *love*, are so frequently linked together. Many of us have experienced the failure of human love and know the devastation and pain that can bring. God repeatedly assures us that His love will *never* fail.

Jeremiah's words are more than just the record of one man's suffering. They are the inspired truth of God and are there to teach us about this same God in the dark times in our own lives. God is faithful and His love will never fail. This is as true today as it was for Jeremiah centuries ago.

Recently my husband, Peter, came in to where I was working to clarify something he had said to me earlier. As he was leaving, I said, "You don't need to explain yourself to me; I know your heart." And I do. I have utmost confidence in his motives, especially toward me. That's the very attitude that God wants us to have toward Him—confidence in His heart and in His unfailing love. Suffering is often a time when we learn to know the heart of God. We learn to have utmost confidence in His motives toward us and in His desire for our best. God asks us to trust His heart, even when we don't understand His ways.

Years ago my sister's little boy, Jeffrey, died. He had been born with many physical difficulties, requiring multiple complicated surgeries. He had responded remarkably well to them, and we were all encouraged. But one night, with no warning, his liver failed, and we received the unexpected and devastating call that he had died.

What a confusing time! We had believed that God was intervening for Jeffrey and had been so hopeful that he would make it. We had even seen God work out some amazing details on behalf of this precious little boy. And then he died.

At the time of Jeffery's death, God gave me these words—

an expression of my heart in response to events and circumstances that didn't make any sense. They were written as a testimony of the pinpoint of light that I saw in this dark time.

*Dear God, your hand has moved in ways I cannot comprehend.*
*I do not understand at all the sorrow that you send.*
*But Lord, your Word reminds me that now I know in part.*
*Until the day I know in full, Lord, let me trust your heart.*

Recently a friend related this story about a colleague of his who suffered for a time from serious depression. Matt was a popular professor who'd had great impact on the lives of many young people preparing for ministry. How could this be happening? And where was God?

As he asked these hard questions, Matt suddenly sensed the quiet presence of God and this calm assurance, "Look at my eyes, not at my hands." In that moment he felt absolute confidence in the love of his Father. He still didn't understand what God's hands were doing in his life, but he trusted the love that he saw in God's eyes. It is much like what my daughter's experience must have been as I twisted her little foot. She felt pain from my hands, but saw nothing but love in my eyes.

God doesn't always give us answers, but He always gives us assurance. He promises us a love that will never, never fail. We can see it in His eyes and can hear it in His voice. Listen again to the words of Jeremiah 29:11: "'For I know the plans I have for you,' declares the LORD, 'plans to prosper you and not to harm you, plans to give you hope and a future.'"

This verse is often quoted, but its familiarity doesn't diminish the hope it offers as God gives us a peek into His compassionate heart. How many times in suffering do we find ourselves without hope? How many times do we look ahead with fear to an unknown future? God was speaking these words specifically to the nation of Israel, but we know that He never changes. The heart that He revealed to His children then is the same heart that He has toward us now.

Notice that this verse does not promise that everything will be wonderful. It doesn't promise that we'll understand all of God's purposes. It does, however, give us absolute assurance that God knows what He's doing and that what He is doing is for our best.

## GOD CAN ONLY DO RIGHT

This brings us to another, perhaps more difficult, truth about God that we need to learn in our times of suffering. Simply put, it is that God always does what is right. There are times when we bristle against that truth. There are times when His actions seem to contradict His love. How can our particular suffering ever be right? How can a loving God allow this?

We need to keep in mind that most of our suffering is the result of this sin-cursed world in which we live, and God is never the originator of sin. That being true, however, we often struggle with His omnipotence in light of our suffering. If He has the power to intervene, why doesn't He?

Listen to these words from Zephaniah 3:5: "The LORD within her is righteous; *he does no wrong.* Morning by morning he dispenses his justice, and every new day he does not fail" (italics added).

*He does no wrong.* This truth involves our bowing before God as the mysterious Sovereign King. We can never fully understand His ways. We can never fully know His purposes.

His very nature as God means that there will always be parts of Him and His ways that are beyond us. He is God and we are not! He sums this up in Isaiah 55:8 when He declares, "For my thoughts are not your thoughts, neither are your ways my ways." As George MacDonald wrote: "It was never the design of the Lord to explain things to our understanding."[3]

At first this can seem like a spiritual cop-out that lets God off the hook when He doesn't seem to be answering prayer, when healing doesn't come, when a marriage isn't restored. We can just push it all under the big umbrella of God's mysterious side and try to ignore the hurting questions. But, in truth, it is this part of Him that offers us the most hope. He is beyond us. He is so vastly beyond us that His purposes cannot always be understood. He is so beyond us that we can find our peace in not having all the answers.

Think back to when I had to painfully twist my newborn daughter's little foot. I was beyond her in years and understanding. I couldn't explain why I was twisting her foot because of her limitations as a baby. But I knew what she couldn't know—my only motive was love.

God has revealed enough of himself to give us the assurance that no suffering is meaningless or cruel. But He has kept enough hidden to bring us to our knees in worship before One whose ways are higher, finer, more perfect than ours— "as the heavens are higher than the earth" (Isaiah 55:9).

Notice that it doesn't just say that God's ways are different than ours. Different doesn't always mean better. No, this Scripture makes it clear that His ways are "higher" than ours. They are often beyond the reach of our understanding because they are loftier and greater than our minds can comprehend. His ways are not just different, they are infinitely superior.

In recent months I have been counseling a woman whose husband left her for a lifestyle of drinking and partying and other women. Linda (not her real name) has had many questions about her future. Should she wait for him to change? Will God restore her marriage? Will her husband be saved? My consistent response has been to encourage her to look away from what she doesn't know (and can't know) to see what she does know.

I can't answer Linda's questions, but I can assure her of some wonderful truths about her heavenly Father—truths that can sustain her and give her hope. Once again we can learn from Jeremiah. He chose to focus on the things he did know, not on his unanswered questions. And he did know that God's compassions never fail!

Sometimes in situations that seem hopeless and overwhelming we have to make a deliberate choice, as Jeremiah did, to "call to mind" God's love and faithfulness. One morning my husband, Peter, and I stayed in bed much later than usual. Quite frankly, neither of us wanted to get up and face the day. We had just discovered that a Christian man who had been involved in our business had cheated us in a way that almost guaranteed our failure. Our concerns about the business were dwarfed by the hurt caused by the actions of this man who was our brother and, we thought, our friend. And so we lay there, dreading the moment when we would have to finally get up and face the day.

As we struggled to deal with our hurt, we began to call to mind Scripture after Scripture of encouragement. I began to recite the familiar and comforting Twenty-third Psalm. Peter joined me. Then we shared verse after verse, reminding each other of God's faithfulness and love. We "grazed" on His

Word, finding the nourishment and help that we so desperately needed. And then we prayed. Not great prayers of mighty faith, but little whispers of childlike dependence. We reached our hands upward and placed them in His mighty, loving, nail-scarred hand. Then we were able to get up and face our day.

I have discovered that as life becomes more complicated, my theology becomes simpler. Years ago I joked that I would someday like to write a Christian version of the book *All I Ever Needed to Know I Learned in Kindergarten*; I would call it *All I Ever Needed to Know I Learned in Beginner's Church*.

It is often the simple, uncomplicated truths that sustain us during the complex times of life. "Jesus loves me, this I know." That alone is enough. Jesus, my Redeemer, the One who has triumphed over death and hell, who is even now interceding on my behalf, loves me! It is a love that cannot fail, that cannot cease, and that "will not let me go!"

Simple, yes, but powerful because it is absolute truth. It becomes that on which we can place our feet when all around is sinking sand. I have known that Jesus loves me since those early days in Beginner's Church, but I have learned the reality of that truth in suffering. We don't need to have all the answers. We don't need to understand all the great issues of theology. But we do need to know our God, for He is our only hope.

## KNOWING WHO WHEN WE DON'T KNOW WHY

Suffering is often a confusing time spiritually. Why doesn't God heal when He can? Why did God allow this to happen? Why doesn't God change my circumstances? We are often baffled and confused by what we perceive to be God's actions, or lack of action, on our behalf. Whatever the specific question, it comes down to one agonizing word: Why?

We may never know the "whys," but we can know the "Who." We can begin to know in a deeply personal way the truths about God's phenomenal nature—His unfailing love, His great faithfulness. And through this knowledge we find, just as Peter promised, unlimited grace and peace.

To read the autobiography of J. Hudson Taylor is to understand suffering on a whole new level. His list could almost rival Paul's. Yet hear what he has to say:

> And how blessedly He did lead me on and provide for me I can never, never tell. My faith was not untried; it often, often failed, and I was so sorry and ashamed of the failure to trust such a FATHER. But, oh! I was learning to know Him. I would not even then have missed the trial. He became so near, so real, so intimate.[4]

That experience can be available to all of us in our suffering. He can truly become so near, so real, so intimate.

This chapter began with these words from Jeremiah: "I will give them a heart to know me." Don't miss this gift because it's wrapped in suffering. That wrapping holds one of the most precious gifts that suffering can offer—the sweetness of knowing our God.

CHAPTER 3

# The Sweetness of His Care

*"For your heavenly Father knows that*
*you need all these things."*
MATTHEW 6:32 NKJV

WHEN I FIRST THOUGHT about writing this chapter, I looked forward to sharing all the wonderful stories of God's care in the small details of life and in the overwhelming times of need, but I imagined myself writing this from the vantage point of looking back, sharing from the ease of one who has "come through" and can report on the journey.

However, that is not the case. I find myself, instead, writing "in the midst" while clinging to my mustard seed of faith, standing at the base of an insurmountable mountain. But our mountain-moving God is faithful. He does hear and He does provide, and I trust my own heart will be encouraged and strengthened as we review God's faithfulness and provision as we once again face great and immediate needs.

I have often said that it is good to have times when we are needy. (I never said that it was easy or fun—just good.) Almost all the stories of great saints, both in the Bible and in Christian literature, include times of need, and never in any of those stories has God failed. In an old book on answers to prayer I found this wonderful quote: "I have never heard of God failing anyone yet and I don't plan to be the first."

We are so encouraged when we read of God's provision and faithfulness in the lives of others. But it is during our own times of need that we grow even more in our personal understanding of God, the loving and faithful Father, as we experience firsthand His provision and care. Our neediness provides an opportunity to learn to know our God better and to see Him revealed in our own circumstances in practical and specific ways. So as we consider the sweetness of God's care, I want to begin by sharing some stories of His material provision.

## WHAT'S FOR BREAKFAST?

One morning years ago when I was a pastor's wife in Buffalo, New York, I had gotten my older two children fed and off to school. I had divided up the last of the cereal for their breakfast and had some milk left, but nothing else—no bread for toast, no eggs—nothing. My husband had already left for the day and I had no money and no car. The one thing I did have, however, was a toddler still in bed. Thankfully he had slept unusually late, but would, without a doubt, wake up very hungry.

I sat down to spend my quiet time with the Lord and had just begun to read my Bible when the doorbell rang. (I hadn't even gotten around to praying yet.) I went to the door and there stood a man from our church who had never come to our house before. He was holding two grocery bags. He thrust these at me and in his usual abrupt manner said, "Just take these. Don't ask any questions—just take 'em," and he turned just as abruptly and left.

By the time Steven woke up I had eight boxes of cereal lined up across our kitchen floor. Steven didn't just have cereal; he had his choice of cereal. When he came downstairs, I took him by the hand and said, "Steven, look what God did for you." I don't know if he fully understood, but I did, and I have never enjoyed watching a four year old eat cereal more than at that moment.

A postscript to this story: I have often joked that there was not one box of "junk" cereal among them. I guess that shows us God's preference.

### YELLOW WOULD BE NICE

At that time we were serving a wonderful and loving church that provided as best they could for us, but things were still tight. Nowhere was that more evident than in my thread-bare bathroom towels. Around the same time as the cereal incident, we were planning to host a guest speaker for the church, and while the towels were fine for us, they were an embarrassment to offer to guests. And so I "made my request known." Actually, I did more than that. I added a PS to my request and in almost a whisper said, "And, Lord, yellow would be nice."

A couple of days later someone arrived at my door with— you guessed it—beautiful *yellow* towels. I had not shared our need with anyone, so you can imagine the rejoicing that took place when I told the woman who brought the towels about my prayer request. A need met, yes, but so much more. I needed the towels, but I also at that time needed the reminder that God loved me enough to even hear my whisper. Not just towels, but yellow towels.

## A Pricey Reproduction

A few years later when we were ministering in a church in Akron, Ohio, an artist in our church offered to reproduce an old family painting for me. I loved this painting, but, being one of seven children, I realized the odds of ever having it passed on to me were rather slim. The perfect solution was to have someone paint a copy of it, and John readily agreed to do this.

I repeatedly asked John about the cost, and he repeatedly said with a reassuring smile that I was not to worry about it. And so he painted a wonderful, perfect reproduction. I was thrilled when he presented it to me, and then I saw that it came with a bill for $200.00. For a pastor's wife on a tight budget, it might as well have been $2,000.00. And so I went to my heavenly Father with the need.

The next Sunday night my husband used the fact that I had lost a contact lens down our drain in a sermon illustration. What that could have been illustrating I can't remember, but he made his point with that little story and went on with his sermon.

Later, a wonderful friend of mine in our church came up to me and handed me an envelope. She said that it was money to replace my missing lens. The check was for a much larger amount than it would cost to replace my contact, but when I tried to give the excess amount back to her, she just quietly said, "Well, that's how much the Lord told me to give you, so He must know you need it for something." Yes, He did! The amount over the cost of the lens was enough to pay for the painting.

## DUTY VERSUS A DREAM

When we were serving our third church, in Syracuse, New York, I faced a far less serious need. Yet sometimes it is those little needs that become wonderful reminders of how personal God is and how aware He is of even the smallest details of our lives.

In this instance, I realized that I needed to get control of certain areas of my life as a homemaker. Balancing full-time ministry and full-time family took organization, and I was a little short in that area so I made some adjustments and some plans. The problem was that to become my new organized self required buying some things for the house and there was no money for extras. The very week that I was thinking about getting started on this, I received a letter from a man in our church, someone I barely knew. He had felt the urging of the Lord to send me a check for $50.00. He was very specific that this check was for *me* to use as I needed.

Now for a confession: I am bona fide bibliophile and I have always had this dream of someone giving me money and saying that I could only spend it at a Christian bookstore. And so I sat with that check in my hand and indulged my dream— $50.00 and a Christian bookstore! It wasn't long, however, before I was brought back to reality and the reminder of just why God had sent me that money. So to Kmart I went. I purchased everything I had on my list, and the cost came within pennies of the amount that had been given to me.

Now for the amazing epilogue to this story: That same

week my husband officiated at a wedding. They paid him in a most unusual way, giving him a gift certificate for our local Christian bookstore in the amount of $50.00. He handed it to me and said, "Here, you might as well have this." I didn't argue. The same God who cares about the most mundane areas of our lives also spoils us occasionally by giving us our secret heart's desires.

## THE ANSWER CAME FIRST

The backdrop of my next God-provision story is the tragic loss of my marriage. At that time, I was fifty years old, and I felt equipped to do nothing other than be a pastor's wife, but the pastor was no longer a pastor nor was he my husband.

I have so many stories of God's faithfulness during that period of time, but one that stands out has to do with a financial need that I didn't know I had. One day I received a check in the mail for a substantial amount of money from some close friends of mine. (The love that surrounded me from the family of God at that time was precious beyond words and is a story in itself.) As I stood holding this check, I said, "Lord, you have been so good that I don't even need this check. I don't understand why you have given this to me." I remember being even a little embarrassed at receiving it because the Lord had provided so well that I truly didn't have a need. I was receiving a small monthly amount from my former husband and had found a job. That, along with loving gifts from friends, left me well cared for. So I was puzzled by this particular check. However, the next day I received a phone call saying that the money from my former husband would not be coming. So God had provided before I even knew that I had a need.

During that same period of time I became ill with mono-nucleosis. Now when you're fifty and have just experienced a time of total upheaval and change, mono hits hard. That was the end of my very short career working in a dentist's office and the beginning of a long stay in bed.

I stayed with my sister while I was recovering, but I still had rent, electric, and other obligations. One day as I was balancing my checkbook I said to my sister, "I don't know how God does math, but I keep taking money out and it just doesn't seem to get lower."

During that time, even without a job, I was always able to pay my bills. God still keeps oil jars full.

### LOAVES AND FISHES

I don't want to make it sound like God's faithfulness means that we will never face financial hardships. In recent years, Peter and I have gone through some difficult times financially due to the struggles with our business. Actually, "difficult times financially" is to put it mildly. We've experienced times of severe need, but, oh, the stories that have come out of this period of time.

One is particularly precious to me because it was a specific answer to a prayer of our teen-age daughter. That day we had counted out the remaining change in our household (after checking under couch cushions and in coat pockets) and had a little over $12.00. I held it in my hands and said to our children, "This is our loaves and fishes. We will give it to God and ask Him to bless it and multiply it."

We gave our daughter $5.00 to put gas in the car on her way to work. Morgan worked at a restaurant that specializes in fish sandwiches—a favorite of her father's. Obviously, there had not been money for eating out or splurging on fish sand-wiches in awhile.

When Morgan got to work, she expressed a wish to God. It wasn't even a specific prayer. She just expressed to God her desire to be able to get her father a fish sandwich. At the end of her shift, a waitress came up to Morgan and said, "We have this extra sandwich left over. Do you want it?"

Did she want it? Did she ever! That had never happened before (or again), and Morgan arrived home, in tears, holding a fish sandwich as if it were the Holy Grail. She said, "Look what God did for me!" We all got a little teary. (Later I said jokingly that God has always been partial to bread and fish and that it was a good thing she hadn't asked for a cheese-burger.) Morgan's faith took one giant step forward that night.

## THAT HEAVENLY COFFEE

Another wonderful example of God's care from that same period of time has to do with coffee. My husband is a great fan of a certain donut shop's coffee and would get a cup each morning for the start of his workday. Now, as a matter of thrift, I made him his coffee each morning and, while he never com-plained, I knew that I couldn't really compete with his old favorite.

One morning I realized that we were just about out of cof-fee, but we only had enough money to get a couple of things that I needed for the kids' lunches. I didn't say anything to my husband about the coffee, but I did say plenty to my heavenly Father as I poured out my heart on behalf of Peter's morning coffee.

Later that day, Peter went to a discount grocery store where we frequently shop to get what I needed for the kids. As he went through the line to pay for his purchases, which came to about $2.50, the cashier said, "We're giving this out free today," and handed him a bag of—you guessed it—coffee. Not a little packet, but a twelve-ounce bag! He came home, handed it to me, and said, "This was really weird. They were giving out these free bags of coffee today." I immediately burst into tears.

When I explained the situation to Peter, we both stood there in amazement and awe. I have to tell you, in all the years I have shopped at that store, I have never known them (before or since) to give out anything free. And yet, on this particular day they gave out free twelve-ounce bags of coffee. I love to think of all the other people who got in on our blessing!

Was it hard to not have enough money for coffee or fish sandwiches? Of course. But think of what we would have missed. And think of what our children would have missed. They have seen a God who can be trusted and who cares about even the small details of our lives. No Sunday school lesson or church sermon can match that.

## DEEPER THAN MY DEPTHS

God's material provision is wonderful, but we often struggle with needs that go far beyond the material realm. One day I woke up not just in the midst but in the depths—a terrible place to be. We were waiting for the other shoe to drop with our business, and the reality of our circumstances came crashing in around me, to the point where my own emotional weariness left me incapable of crawling out.

I picked up my Bible and opened it to my reading for the day: "Out of the depths I cry to you, O LORD; O Lord, hear my voice. Let your ears be attentive to my cry for mercy" (Psalm 130:1–2). These words were the echo of my own heart. I might not be able to crawl out of my circumstances, but I could cry out. And I did. And God in His faithfulness heard my cry for mercy.

A few days earlier I had watched *The Hiding Place,* the story of the experiences of Corrie ten Boom during World War II. In the midst of circumstances far worse than mine, amid the horrors of a Nazi concentration camp, Corrie's sister Betsie ten Boom proclaimed: "There is no pit so deep that God is not deeper still." Now, as God reminded me of those words, I was so encouraged. I did not have to reach up to God. He was underneath me, even in this deep pit of despair and discouragement. I also began to recall the words of an old hymn by A. B. Simpson:

> *Art thou sunk in depths of sorrow*
> *Where no arm can reach so low?*
> *There is One whose arms almighty*
> *Reach beyond thy deepest woe.*
> *God th'Eternal is thy refuge,*
> *Let it stay thy wild alarms,*
> *Underneath thy deepest sorrow*
> *Are the everlasting arms . . .*
>
> *Underneath us, O how easy;*
> *We have not to mount on high,*
> *But to sink into His fullness,*
> *And in trustful weakness lie.*
> *And we find our humbling failures*
> *Save us from the strength that harms!*
> *We may fail, but underneath us*
> *Are the everlasting arms.*

Underneath me were the everlasting arms! I did not have to "mount on high," but could "sink into His fullness and in trustful weakness lie." God didn't demand that I get out of the pit. He didn't look down from His lofty heights and scold me for being there. He didn't even reach down to pull me up. He simply went deeper and held out His loving and everlasting arms.

The way out of the depths is not always up. Sometimes it's down in "trustful weakness" into His arms.

## A New Friend

During the time that we were going through our business problems, Peter and I visited Brooklyn Tabernacle in New York on Easter Sunday. I sat beside a woman, Sandra, who was such a blessing to me as we talked and shared and then prayed together before the service began. She gave me a copy of a new CD by the Brooklyn Tabernacle Choir that we enjoyed on our trip home that night.

Soon after Easter I wrote to Sandra to thank her for her encouragement and for the CD and to let her know how the Lord had blessed our whole family through the music. I didn't hear back from her, although I didn't really expect to.

A few months later, on a Sunday, I was fighting discouragement and fear—again. For a time things had looked hopeful and encouraging for the business, but finally the other shoe had dropped with a loud crash! That morning before church I prayed and specifically asked the Lord for something personal from Him that day. I went to church confident that there would be something (a song, a word of Scripture) that I would know was especially for me. Something that would minister to my needy heart.

It was a good service with good music, but no special word for me. I was quiet on the way home, wondering why God had seemed to ignore my plea. As we approached our house, I noticed a package by our mailbox. We were all surprised because it had not been there the day before when we got our mail and, as we all well know, the post office doesn't deliver on Sunday. I walked over to get it and saw that it was addressed to me personally.

If it had been postmarked "Heaven" I wouldn't have been surprised, and while the return address was Brooklyn, it was still heaven-sent. Inside the package were four tapes of sermons by Pastor Jim Cymbala, three tapes of the choir (none of which we had), three books, and a couple of pamphlets. What a personal reminder from God that He had heard my prayer. But it gets even better.

The next day I put in one of Pastor Cymbala's tapes and listened in amazement as his sermon unfolded. If the Holy Spirit himself had prepared a sermon that morning for me, it could not have been more timely and encouraging. (What's even more remarkable is that the Holy Spirit had prepared that sermon for me weeks, maybe even months, before.) I listened with tears streaming down my face.

When my husband returned from work I shared what an encouragement the tape had been and expressed the hope that we could listen to it together sometime. He said, "Come on!" and we got in the car and drove around for about forty minutes listening and weeping together. As the sermon concluded, Pastor Cymbala gave an altar call, and I said to Peter, "We're going forward!" He took my hand and said, "I know we are." And there in our car we responded in a deliberate choice of faith to the truth of God's Word. The sermon, by the way, was "Explanations Come Later."

Our God is so faithful, and He used one of His faithful children to minister to us. I think so often of Sandra's timing in sending that package. How sensitive she was to the urging of the Spirit, and God used her to answer my prayer for something personal from Him. (Still no explanation about how we got a package on Sunday, but "explanations come later.")

Some of my most intimate times with God have come as a result of my deepest emotional struggles. God not only understands our infirmities, He also understands "the feelings of our infirmities" (Hebrews 4:15). I have heard many sermons on the physical suffering of Christ while He was here on earth, but Scripture clearly indicates that He also experienced a depth of suffering on the emotional level to which none of us can possibly relate. But it is that very depth of suffering that enables Him to relate to each and every one of us, no matter how severe our struggle.

## A Wonderful PS

Since writing this chapter, our worst fears were realized. Despite a valiant effort by my husband, we lost our business. The ripple effect of that was that we also lost our home. Yet God's peace during those days was amazing. And even more amazing was the way He provided for us. It is too long and complicated to explain the "planning ahead" that took place on the part of God to bring all of this about, but trust me when I say it was anticipated years ahead by our Father and His provision was already in place.

Another factor in all of this was our son, who was still

living at home. I asked the Lord to allow us to stay in our home until he graduated so as not to add to the upheaval in his life. When we were served the notice to vacate our home, we saw that the date we were to leave was the day after his graduation. We were so thankful for God's grace, but that still left us with the question of where we would go.

In an amazing turn of events that had God's fingerprints all over it, a house became available to us, rent free. at exactly the time when we would need it. In fact, the closing was moved up for the couple vacating the house, so the timing was perfect. We helped them move out, and they helped us move in.

I wish you could see our home. Our things look like they have always belonged here—it's perfect for us. A friend left these verses for me after being here for a visit: "LORD, you have assigned me my portion and my cup; you have made my lot secure. The boundary lines have fallen for me in pleasant places; surely I have a delightful inheritance" (Psalm 16:5–6). He truly has.

An additional note of praise is that we are now able to pay rent—further evidence of God's provision against all odds.

Eugenia Price states, "My need is the most glorious possession I have outside of Christ Himself."[1] It is our needs that draw us to the all-sufficient One and allow us to experience firsthand the sweetness of His personal and loving care.

CHAPTER 4

# The Sweetness of Surrender

*Let him do to me whatever seems good to him.*

2 SAMUEL 15:26

"LET HIM DO to me whatever seems good to him." The context of these words spoken by David makes them intensely meaningful. He was fleeing for his life—again. This time it wasn't Saul who was chasing him, but his own son Absalom.

God had promised David that he would be Israel's king, but for a long time that had seemed impossible. The road to the throne had been a difficult one. King Saul had threatened David's life; he had gathered the armies of Israel and chased David, determined to destroy this threat to his throne. For years David spent much of his time either on the run or hiding in caves with his group of misfit followers. Finally God's promise was fulfilled and David was established as Israel's king.

Long live the king? Not if his son Absalom had his way,

and once again David was running for his life. It was then that David made this incredible declaration: "Let him [God] do to me whatever seems good to him."

The context of my reading David's words also made them intensely meaningful for me. I was at a point where I was baffled by God. Circumstances seemed to contradict all of God's promises. David's situation took on great meaning as I wondered what David's emotions were as he was fleeing for his life. Was he struggling with any of the same emotions and questions that were mine? Was he angry? Was he frustrated with God? Did he feel that God had failed him?

He was supposed to be king. God had *promised* him he would be king. It wasn't fair. It wasn't right. It was even worse because he was being threatened by his own flesh and blood; the child he had held and loved was now threatening his kingdom and his life.

We aren't told what David was feeling, but we are told what David said. And in his response to these circumstances we see surrender—absolute surrender to God and His purposes.

The remarkable thing we notice here is that David didn't see himself as being at the mercy of Absalom. Take a minute to think about the significance of that for our own lives. Many times our suffering is caused by another person. We are treated unfairly, or someone else's sin causes us great pain and heartache. Sometimes it is someone close to us—someone we love.

Listen to the words of David in Psalm 55:12–14: "If an enemy were insulting me, I could endure it; if a foe were raising himself against me, I could hide from him. But it is you . . . my companion, my close friend, with whom I once enjoyed sweet fellowship as we walked with the throng at the house of God."

David understood and expressed the added pain we experience when the source of our suffering is someone close to us: "But it is you . . ." I understand David's emotions. I have felt the same anguish. When someone we love and trust fails us or betrays us, our pain is even deeper.

And so it is even more remarkable when we see David, in the midst of what had to be great personal grief, responding by surrendering to God's purposes. And his response teaches us a vitally important lesson that we can apply to our own lives: This was ultimately not about David and Absalom. It was about David and God. David chose to yield—not to his son's evil intentions, but to a God who knew best. He surrendered to God; he didn't abdicate to Absalom.

### Three Choices

At times of suffering we have three choices: We can rebel against what has happened to us and become angry and bitter. We can resign ourselves to the inevitable with a sense of helplessness. Or we can yield to the purposes of a loving heavenly Father and discover the sweetness of that surrender.

It's important here to make a distinction between resignation and surrender. Resignation says, "Oh, well!" Surrender says, "Okay!" Only surrender offers hope. Only surrender leads to peace.

David's response was not one of resignation. We don't sense that he is saying, "Que sera, sera, whatever will be, will be. I can't control the outcome of this anyhow, so, God, do what You will." We see, instead, the heart of someone who had learned to trust the plans and purposes of God. His life had taught him the truth expressed in Psalm 18:30: "As for God, his way is perfect." David could confidently face a situation like this with all of its uncertainties because he also believed that it was God who "makes my way perfect." (Psalm 18:32).

Andrew Murray commented on the same thing when he wrote: "It is infinite consequence that we not only submit, because we are compelled to, but because we lovingly and joyfully consent to be in the hands of our blessed Father."[1]

How can we surrender to suffering? We can't if we see suffering as coming from the hands of others, or if we see ourselves at the mercy of our circumstances or fate. In *The Christian's Secret of a Happy Life*, Hannah Whitall Smith writes, "If our Father permits a trial to come, it must be because the trial is the sweetest and best thing that could happen to us, and we must accept it with thanks from His dear hand."[2]

When I was little and questioning the ways of God in my young life, my mother took my small hand in hers and traced her finger in gentle circles around and around the palm of my hand as she said these words to me: "In the center of the circle of the will of God I stand. There can be no second causes, *all* must come from His dear hand." I didn't fully understood the significance of those words at that time, but I was to hear them many times over the years, and I watched that truth lived out before me in the life of my mother.

Hannah Whitall Smith illustrates this truth with the example of a mother giving a child much-needed medicine. Those of us who have had to do that know that the child seldom takes the medicine eagerly or even willingly. Why then do we insist on torturing our children in this way? There is one reason and one reason alone: We desire what is best for our child, rather than what is immediately enjoyable.

Many parents remember holding down a screaming child while a nurse took blood or gave them a shot. Cruel? Of course not. Does it seem cruel to the child? Perhaps at the moment, but we do what needs to be done for their ultimate good.

Listen to the clear application that Mrs. Smith makes: "The human beings around us are often the bottles that hold our medicine, but it is our Father's hand of love that pours out the medicine, and compels us to drink it."[3]

## IS GOD IN EVERYTHING?

This truth was brought home to me in a very dramatic way. One of my greatest joys in ministry was a Wednesday night Bible study that I led in our church in Syracuse, New York. What a wonderful group of women! Over the years we had laughed and cried together. We had prayed for one another and shared each other's heartaches. We had seen women come to know the Lord and watched them grow spiritually through the Word.

I remember a new Christian coming in one week so excited. "This stuff really works!" she said. "I mean, when you do like the Bible says, it really works!" What a privilege God gave me to be a part of that group.

One Wednesday night we were to begin a study in the book of Colossians. As I began to prepare, I immediately skipped over the introductory remarks to get to the "good stuff." But God very clearly brought me back to Paul's greeting (1:1). I read it once, and again moved on to the next verses. After all, what can you really find exciting to share from "Paul, an apostle of Christ Jesus by the will of God, and Timothy our brother"? But God once again led me back to the very beginning of the book. So we began our study that night on "Paul, an apostle of Christ Jesus by the will of God." My question to those ladies was this: If we are walking with the Lord, can we say, no matter what description follows our name, that it is "by the will of God?" Obviously, it is easy to understand how Paul could say that. After all, he was Paul, an apostle of Christ Jesus. But what if what follows our name is not so wonderful? Can we say, for instance, "Bonnie, wife of an alcoholic husband by the will of God"?

This was not a simple topic. We were basically asking the same question posed by Hannah Whitall Smith in her chapter entitled "Is God in Everything?"⁴

Our conclusion was that He is. If we, as children of God, are walking in obedience to Him, then we can believe that He allows only what is for our best. That was the lesson I taught, but for me the test came a few days later.

That Wednesday night was my last night with those ladies and that Bible study. In the next few days, everything that followed my name changed as the truth about my husband's hidden life was revealed. Later, I wrote these words to my Bible study group:

Dear Ladies:

It was three weeks ago tonight that I was with you. I never imagined that it would be my last time to share with you. How quickly our life can change. Do you remember what we talked about that night? I do— vividly—because God has allowed me to live what I taught you that night. We talked about being able to say under *any* circumstances that we are what we are by the will of God—no matter what that might be. There are many things that follow my name now that are hard. Harder still is what doesn't follow my name. I can no longer say, "I, Esther, pastor's wife," and even more, I can no longer say, "I, Esther, pastor's wife of this wonderful church." Let me say that I am grateful for the ten years that God has privileged me to be able to say that, but I will deeply miss this church and, in particular, "my" ladies. You have meant so much to me and I want to thank you for what you have added to my life.

Is God in everything? How easily I assured you of that three weeks ago. How often the Lord has reminded me of that in these days. Yes, He is in everything! By the time these circumstances have touched me, they have become God's will. Let me quote again from *The Christian's Secret of a Happy Life*. "The human beings around us are often the bottles that hold our medicine, but it is our Father's hand *of love* that pours out the medicine and compels us to drink it." There is tremendous comfort in that for me now.

You are my ladies and we have always had a wonderful openness among us. And so in that spirit I will ask you to please pray for me now. These are difficult days and the medicine is bitter, but I fully trust the One who gives it. I will miss you. I will never forget the wonderful times we had together, laughing and crying and learning. They will always be some of my most cherished memories. God bless all of you. And remember, He is in *everything!!*

## A NEW PICTURE

It is so important that I again stress the truth that God is never the originator of sin. He never delights in sin's effects and devastation, but neither is He surprised by it. He "goes before," which means that in anticipation of the sorrow that we will experience in this life, He has already made all the provision necessary for us. He is already in our future forming even the sins of others into His perfect will for our lives. How can we not surrender to a God who loves us so much? People fail. God never does.

When my children were little we played a game called "The Scribble Game." It originated on a long car trip. (In those days all car trips seemed long, and this may have been something I thought up to avoid hearing "The Bear Went over the Mountain"—again.) One person scribbled on a piece of paper and then passed it to the next person who had to take those scribbled lines and create a picture. As I'm sure you can imagine, this produced very little great art but much hilarity.

There was a time when my "picture" was exactly how I wanted it. I was a wife, a mother, and a pastor's wife at a church that I loved. It was a beautiful picture. Then the black lines of sin were scribbled all over my beautiful picture and it looked like it was ruined forever. "But there is a God in heaven," and He had anticipated every one of those lines. Not one of them surprised Him. Not only did He know that they would be on my picture, but He had wonderful plans to use those very lines to create a new picture—a masterpiece. It looks different from the original, but it has been drawn by my loving heavenly Father.

A verse that is often quoted to people who are suffering as a result of the sins of others is Genesis 50:20: "You intended to harm me, but God intended it for good." The context of these words is the dramatic story of Joseph's reunion with his brothers. What makes this reunion so unusual is the reason for the separation.

If you recall, Joseph was viewed as a favored son by his

father and as a conceited, spoiled brat by his brothers. His brothers' resentment of him simmered until it resulted in a hateful plot. They would get rid of him. Originally the plan was to kill him, but greed was added to hatred and so they sold him to a passing caravan instead.

We pick up the story years later when a wealthy and influential Joseph encounters some needy brothers. When the brothers realize that they are at the mercy of the very one they had harmed, they are filled with terror. And that is the backdrop for these remarkable and oft-quoted words by Joseph: "You intended to harm me, but God intended it for good." In light of the magnitude of the wrong done to him, where did that amazing response come from?

Our answer is found, at least in part, in the names of Joseph's children. We find these words in Genesis 41:51–52: "Joseph named his firstborn Manassah and said, 'It is because God has made me forget all my trouble and all my father's household.' The second son he named Ephraim and said, 'It is because God has made me fruitful in the land of my suffering.'"

The names of Joseph's sons suggest that he had surrendered to God's purposes and recognized God's blessing (sweetness) in the midst of his suffering. I truly believe that Joseph's forgiveness of his brothers could not have happened apart from his surrender to God's purposes. Joseph was able to offer forgiveness because he was able to see his brothers' evil actions as part of God's perfect plan for his life. He understood that God's purposes were greater than his pain and that God's good outweighed his brothers' evil.

Again, let me stress that we never read that God condoned what was done to Joseph. God never condones sin. What Joseph's brothers did was wrong—it was evil. But the amazing truth is that God is never thrown off by our sin. In His hands, even evil acts can become a source of blessing. So Joseph was able to genuinely offer love and forgiveness because he had yielded to God's purposes, even when brought about through the evil intentions of his jealous brothers. Only God!

## LETTING GOD DEFINE GOOD

But not all suffering comes to us through the hands of others. What about suffering that we feel God could have prevented?

I will never forget one of the first times I knelt to pray for a friend of mine who had been diagnosed with a rare and aggressive type of cancer. Glen was in his prime—a successful pastor with a beautiful wife and three young children. As I began to pray, I sensed God's warning: "You may pray for him with empathy and concern, but *do not pity him.*"

I had to humbly confess to God that that's exactly what I was feeling. Poor Glen. Why him? Why now? Why should this happen to a man who was faithfully serving in a successful and growing church? What about his poor family? But God was asking that there should be no pity. Why? Because pity implies that someone else could have chosen better for Glen. Pity implies that God had somehow goofed. Pity cannot partner with surrender.

What God taught me through Glen was that His way is always best. Not always understood. Not always easy. Not always what we would choose. But best! King Nebuchadnezzer learned that truth the hard way and, after a very humbling experience, he declared: "Everything he [God] does is right" (Daniel 4:37). There is no greater basis for surrender.

Scripture is emphatic about this truth. Remember David's

words: "As for God, his way is perfect" (Psalm 18:30). Perfect! That doesn't leave any room for error or poor judgment. Perfect! That doesn't allow for any improvement. Perfect! That means any other way is inferior.

In a wonderful book, *Hidden Rift with God*, William Backus admonishes us that we need to allow God to define good.[5] Our definition would almost always include what is easy and comfortable. God's often doesn't. To surrender is to trust the One whose way is perfect and who alone can make our way perfect, even in suffering. It is to allow God to define good.

A dramatic example of total surrender to God's will is found in the lives of Corrie and Betsie ten Boom. These two middle-aged, single women found themselves facing the horrors of imprisonment in a Nazi concentration camp. Their crime? They had hidden Jews in their home and helped them escape from the Nazis.

The suffering of these women was of a magnitude beyond comprehension for most of us. How could anyone find hope or encouragement in those circumstances? Their secret was that they did not see themselves at the mercy of the Nazis, but rather in the will of their heavenly Father who alone could bring good out of the awful horrors surrounding them.

In the years following the war, Corrie's testimony (Betsie died in the prison camp) had an impact that could only come from her ability to say, "I understand. I was there." History has already shown us the great influence of her life. Eternity will show us more.

### Understanding Rather Than Answers

The prophet Habakkuk gives us another glimpse of surrender in the midst of great difficulties. The book of Habakkuk begins with his questions and complaints about the injustice that he saw all around him and ends with his choice to rejoice.

What changed? What happened that caused him to be joyful? Did God answer his questions and resolve all of his complaints so that he could say, "Oh, I see what you're doing and now I understand"? No, that didn't happen for Habakkuk, and it seldom happens for us.

I think the answer is found in these words: "His ways are eternal" (Habakkuk 3:6). Habakkuk still didn't have answers to all of his questions. He didn't know what God would do to bring resolution to the problems he saw. But he did understand that God's purposes went beyond the immediate—"His ways are eternal." So it didn't matter anymore if there were cattle in the stalls and grapes on the vine. With or without those, Habakkuk chose to surrender to a God who would do what was eternally best.

Often when we are facing times of suffering we are baffled by God's ways. We can't see any clear answers or make sense of our circumstances. But surrender doesn't depend on our ability to understand why. Surrender doesn't wait until everything makes sense. Surrender is only possible because of what we know to be true about the One to whom we surrender.

Paul teaches us this same truth as he offers a wonderful description of God's purposes in Romans 12:2, where he refers to God's will as "good, pleasing, and perfect." The King James Version translates this phrase as "good, and acceptable, and perfect."

Pleasing! Acceptable! The only way that we can find His will acceptable or pleasing is to be surrendered to Him—not to "it" but to Him. Surrender is to join David in saying, "Let him do to me, whatever seems good to him."

Remember, when we do this, we are not just giving in to the inevitable. We are not just accepting whatever fate may have for us. We are not just yielding to circumstances. We are surrendering to a loving heavenly Father who is perfect in His love toward us and who truly knows what is good and perfect. And that is what makes God's purposes—even when they include suffering—acceptable.

Our hope in suffering comes as we remain absolutely surrendered to our loving Father and to His good, and pleasing, and acceptable will. And in that we will find the sweetness that comes from surrender.

## CHAPTER 5

# The Sweetness of Shared Suffering

*Rejoice that you participate in the sufferings of Christ.*

1 PETER 4:13

EVERY YEAR ON December 22 a group of middle-aged men meet to commemorate an event that happened years ago. They come from different places and different walks of life, but they share one bond that is greater than all of their differences. They are the sixteen survivors of the plane that crashed in the Andes on October 13, 1972. Twelve people died in the crash. The survivors lost hope as the days passed and others began to die from starvation and the harsh environment. Finally, two of the men decided to attempt to cross the huge mountains to find help. On December 22, after seventy-two days, the world learned that there were sixteen survivors. Their story is a dramatic and gripping saga of a fight to stay alive in a merciless environment.

So what is it that unites these men after all these years? What is it that draws them back year after year to spend this particular day together? Is it the memories of their past glory days as rugby players? Is it to recapture the camaraderie of their youth? No, it is their shared experience of suffering that draws them. It has forged a bond of understanding between them that time cannot diminish.

## THE COMMON BOND OF SUFFERING

Some months after my husband initially disclosed his hidden life, I was feeling overwhelmed as the ripple effects and consequences of his sin continued to break over my life. I remember sitting in a wooded area by the banks of a quiet stream. The setting was idyllic and peaceful. My heart was not. I was experiencing emotional pain so deep that it felt like my heart would never heal. I felt crushed by the weight of it. In those moments of personal anguish my Savior brought this thought to mind: "I have not asked anything of you that I haven't done for you." I was stunned by the truth of those quiet words.

He was reminding me that we had a common bond in suffering. He too had experienced betrayal and rejection. He too had been misunderstood and misrepresented. He too had suffered because of someone else's sin. While my suffering could never come close to the injustice and agony Christ experienced, in those moments I felt the wonderful bond of shared suffering with Him.

Those moments changed me forever. Christ not only understood my pain, He was inviting me to share in His. I began to weep, not for myself, but for my Savior, for all He had willingly endured for me. Christ chose to suffer. I didn't. I would never have chosen this! And suddenly the love that would prompt such a choice washed over my own pain and brought relief. My Savior and I were one in a new way. We shared the common bond of suffering.

The apostle Paul implies that this kind of shared bond is part of knowing Christ when he says, "I want to know Christ and the power of his resurrection *and* the fellowship of sharing in his sufferings" (Philippians 3:10). It's not enough to just know *about* Christ's suffering. We need to know the fellowship of sharing in His sufferings. As we allow our own pain to help us identify with the suffering Savior, we are brought into fellowship with Him, and that, even when accomplished through suffering, is always sweet.

## FELLOWSHIP IS MORE THAN A PARTY

*Fellowship* is a quaint word that conjures up images of church dinners and Sunday school socials, and is sometimes used as a sanctimonious word for *party*. But in actuality, fellowship is a meaningful word that denotes companionship between people who share much in common.

The first relationship between God and man was one of fellowship. In the beginning Adam knew unhindered fellowship with the Creator God. They walked in oneness together in the garden along paths designed by God for His beloved creation. Imagine the pureness of the love expressed between them. Imagine having God in all His beauty and majesty as your walking partner and companion. Then imagine losing that! If grief is proportionate to the value of what is lost, imagine Adam's grief. Imagine living the rest of your life with an awareness of that loss—a longing that could never again be filled, a joy that could never again be known, an innocence that could never again be felt. Every day there had to be that sense of longing for the fellowship that was lost.

Could it be that as Adam's descendants we have inherited that longing? Could it be that there is a part of us that senses a faint and distant memory of what was and longs for it once more? As descendants of Adam we share in his sin, but perhaps we also share in his intense longing to once again have fellowship with the Creator.

Thankfully, God came again to a garden and offered to "bear our grief and carry our sorrow"—a sorrow so great that it has been felt by every child of Adam throughout history. God carried that sorrow and made it His own on the cross so that we could once again take garden walks together along paths designed by the almighty Creator for His beloved. The truth is that the Holy God also missed those walks in the garden. A beautiful picture of God's desire for fellowship with us is found in His words in Revelation 3:20 where He says, "Here I am! I stand at the door and knock. If anyone hears my voice and opens the door, I will come in and eat with him, and he with me."

The horror of sin was that fellowship with the Almighty was destroyed. It was sin that broke that fellowship, but it was suffering that restored it. And if we are to truly enjoy that fellowship with God once again, we must be willing to share in His suffering.

When the sixteen survivors of the Andes crash get together each year, it is not a casual get-together. Nando Parrado, author of *Miracle in the Andes* and one of the two men who climbed through the Andes Mountains for ten days to find help, says this, "When I am together with my fellow survivors, we say in silence all that needs to be said about our time in the mountains."[1] They know the "fellowship of suffering" that goes beyond words.

For us there is so much more ahead than just a yearly get-together. Paul reminds us that "we share in his sufferings in order that we may also share in his glory" (Romans 8:17). Then he goes on to try to give us some idea of the greatness of that glory in comparison to our suffering. His conclusion is that they aren't even worth comparing. Suffering is an investment in future glory, a glory that is beyond our ability to grasp. And that glory will someday be as real as our suffering is today.

## SUFFERING HAPPENS!

The apostle Peter also has something to say about suffering: "Dear friends, do not be surprised at the painful trial you are suffering, as though something strange were happening to you" (1 Peter 4:12). If we had to reduce that to a bumper sticker, it would simply read, "Suffering happens!" And life would certainly endorse that statement.

But then Peter adds some astounding, some might even say absurd, advice: "But rejoice . . ." Who would dare to say that to someone in the midst of personal turmoil or grief? Yet Peter dares, and the reason is found in the next verse: "But rejoice that you participate in the sufferings of Christ" (1 Peter 4:13). Peter wasn't expecting us to never grieve, but he was encouraging us to understand that these "painful trials" include a privilege that can allow us to rejoice through our tears.

I experienced the reality of this that morning by the stream. There isn't any human suffering that isn't understood by our Savior. There isn't any pain or heartache that He hasn't felt. He longs to use our suffering, in whatever form it may take, to draw us back into the garden to walk with Him in deep and intimate fellowship. What Adam lost is ours once again.

## FEELING SOMEONE ELSE'S PAIN

"Now you are the body of Christ, and each one of you is a part of it" (1 Corinthians 12:27). "If one part suffers, every part suffers with it" (12:26).

I remember a number of years ago feeling a certain envy for those women who had been privileged to care for the physical body of Christ. His mother Mary had nurtured Him in His childhood. Mary and Martha had Him in their home as a guest and fed Him and cared for Him. And Mary, in a gesture of grateful love and deep worship, poured perfume on His feet and wiped them with her hair. Imagine being one of those women who was in the actual physical presence of Christ.

As I sat thinking about this, the Lord gently reminded me that I have the same privilege today as those women did so many years ago as I care for His body—the church. Scripture makes it clear that Christ's body now is His church and that it is complete with all the parts, from head to toes. As we care for one another in the body, we care for Christ. That's why He also says, "I tell you the truth, whatever you did for one of the least of these brothers of mine, you did for me" (Matthew 25:40). When Christ says, "I tell you the truth," He wants us to understand that this is more than a clever metaphor. It is Truth. His children make up His body!

One of the sweet sides of suffering for a child of God is the care that is experienced within the body. When a part of our physical body suffers, we often see other parts compensate as they share in the suffering. God made our bodies to function that way because it's what we need. God made the body of Christ to function that way also because it's what we need.

During my years in ministry I saw so many wonderful examples of this. And in my recent years of suffering, I have experienced this on a personal level. The tragedy is that sometimes the body of Christ fails miserably to fulfill this important ministry to one another.

I just spoke to a friend of mine. Judy has been having a hard morning. In addition to the grief of recently losing both of her parents, she is packing up her home of over twenty years to move to another state. That means leaving behind her children and her adorable grandchildren. Her husband has already moved there ahead of her, so she is feeling very alone in her grief. She told me that when she shared all of this through her tears with a friend from church, her friend responded by rebuking her for her selfishness. Yes, you read that right! The response of her friend was to chastise her. That left Judy feeling more alone than ever in her grief.

## The Gift of "Efu"

I found a wonderful expression of shared suffering when visiting a missionary friend in Africa. A man came to her door and began to tell her something with great emotion. She was obviously moved by what he was telling her and would say repeatedly, "Efu, efu." I couldn't understand a word of what was being said, but when my friend said "efu" I understood that she was expressing her concern and empathy for what he was saying.

That is what Judy needed from her friend. Judy's friend needed to "efu" her—to share in her suffering and to cry with her. But instead of lightening Judy's grief, she loaded her down with guilt. She not only missed a wonderful opportunity to "hurt with those who are hurting," but she poured salt in an already wounded heart. How different this is from what we are called to be to one another in the body of Christ.

I had a wonderful "efu" experience a number of years after the breakup of my first marriage. The pain of losing my marriage of thirty years was horrific for me, but it was also overwhelming for my grown children. They came from an extended family where "this had never happened" and from an immediate family where "this could never happen." But it did, and they were left with deep sorrow of their own which blinded them to mine. As a result, we had some very rough times.

A number of years later when one of my sons was visiting me and we were having a quiet evening just enjoying being together, he suddenly said, "Mom, tell me what it was like for you when you found out about Dad." I was amazed at the request and began to tell him in very general terms how difficult that had been.

He listened carefully and probed deeper. He wanted to know my pain. He wanted to share my pain.

Let me interject here that in an attempt to spare my children even greater heartache I had not told them a lot of the specifics regarding their father's sin. He would no longer be my husband, but he would remain their father and I felt there was simply no need for them to know. They knew enough. But that night Steven needed to know more, and so little by little I shared my story.

It was an amazing night as Steven wept with me and

insisted on sharing in my suffering. At the end, my man-child held me in his arms as we cried together. As we finished, my son thanked me for my honesty and said this, "I need to know how deeply I could hurt someone if I ever failed in this way." He needed to understand my suffering as a guard in his own life. Even today it is impossible to write about this without deep emotion. He will never fully understand the gift that he gave me that night and the healing power of that gift.

Another "efu" moment for me came the summer following my personal upheaval. My "Aunt" Betty (a family friend for many years) had also suffered a year of sorrow with the loss of her husband, my beloved "Uncle" Jack. When we saw each other that summer, we hugged and then both began to cry. After a few minutes, as we held each other and cried, she said, "I'm not crying for me. I'm crying for you." I responded immediately, "Well, I wasn't crying for me. I was crying for you." Then we both began to laugh. It was a moment where we were each sharing in the suffering of the other. What a privilege and what a gift.

## Equipped to "Efu"

Shared suffering is to be a hallmark of the body of Christ. In fact, being part of the same body should make that natural. Paul tells us that the parts of Christ's body "should have equal concern for each other. If one part suffers, every part suffers with it" (1 Corinthians 12:25–26). Scripture calls us to do this, but our own suffering equips us to do this. Listen to Paul's words in 2 Corinthians 1:3–5:

> Praise be to the God and Father of our Lord Jesus Christ,
> the Father of compassion and the God of all comfort,

who comforts us in all our troubles, so that we can comfort those in any trouble with the comfort we ourselves have received from God. For just as the sufferings of Christ flow over into our lives, so also through Christ our comfort overflows.

Look at how Paul identifies God: "the Father of compassion" and "the God of all comfort." What wonderful names! They reveal so much about the nature of God. He is a God of deep feeling and shares with us in our times of suffering. And He calls us to do the same for one another.

A friend of mine once told me about an experience he had when he was a young pastor. He was facing some difficult times in his ministry and was feeling discouraged and overwhelmed. During that period, he was working at his denominational camp for a week where one of the leaders of his denomination was the speaker. One night, after the evening service, when everyone else was enjoying ice cream and fun, he quietly slipped back into the darkened sanctuary and knelt at the altar. He began to weep as he silently poured out his heart to God. As he prayed, he became aware that someone had joined him. It was the speaker. Without saying a word, he slipped an arm around my weeping friend and cried with him. He didn't ask any questions. He didn't offer any counsel. He just wept with him. He entered into his suffering. It was an "efu" moment that brought strength and encouragement to this young pastor. It was one part of the body sharing in the suffering of another part of the body.

Christ privileges us to share in His suffering and to experience the bond that comes through that experience. Then He admonishes us to "go and do likewise."

When we allow the comfort that we've experienced from God to overflow onto the pain of others, we can truly offer them the sweetness of shared suffering—the gift of "efu."

## CHAPTER 6

# The Sweetness of His Comfort

*"I, even I, am he who comforts you."*
ISAIAH 51:12

MY LARGE AND wonderful family had gathered together at a camp to spend some days together, which included the celebration of my parents' fiftieth wedding anniversary.

On Sunday, following the anniversary celebration, we met for our own time of worship—just our immediate family and a few aunts. We older girls dug out one of our old trio numbers to sing. The youngest (twin boys) sang, "May Those Who Come Behind Us Find Us Faithful," while their older sisters cried. Together we sang our father's favorite, "It Is Well with My Soul," and we all cried. (We're a family that laughs easily and cries easily.)

Then my father spoke. I had grown up under my father's preaching and, as a child, I had often tuned him out. I now realized that I had missed some wonderful preaching over the years. On this occasion he spoke about the importance of keeping Christ as the center and focus of all that we do. At one point in his message he urged us not to forget the old hymns and specifically mentioned, "Majestic Sweetness Sits Enthroned." I suspect that the teenage grandchildren sitting there had never heard this hymn. (Many of you may not have either.)

The story picks up again about three months later when I received the startling news of my father's unexpected death. I literally doubled over as if someone had knocked the wind out of me. I was stunned and grief-stricken. It was late at night and I knew that there would be no sleep for me, so I went downstairs to my prayer chair and sat and wept.

My father was a remarkable man and a huge and important part of my life. I couldn't imagine him not being there anymore. At some point, as I sat there engulfed in grief, I thought of my dad's comments a few months earlier and reached for my hymnbook to look up "Majestic Sweetness Sits Enthroned," the old hymn that he had mentioned.

*Majestic sweetness sits enthroned*
*Upon the Saviour's brow;*
*His head with radiant glories crowned,*
*His lips with grace o'erflow.*

*No mortal can with Him compare,*
*Among the sons of men;*
*Fairer is He than all the fair*
*That fill the heavenly train.*

*He saw me plunged in deep distress,*
*He flew to my relief;*

*For me He bore the shameful cross,*
*And carried all my grief.*

*To Him I owe my life and breath,*
*And all the joys I have;*
*He makes me triumph over death,*
*And saves me from the grave.*

*To heaven, the place of His abode,*
*He brings my weary feet;*
*Shows me the glories of my God,*
*And makes my joys complete.*

*Since from His bounty I receive*
*Such proofs of love Divine,*
*Had I a thousand hearts to give,*
*Lord, they should all be Thine.*

As I read these wonderful words—"To heaven, the place of His abode, He brings my weary feet. Shows me the glories of my God, and makes my joy complete"—I sat there in amazement. God had used my dad's own comments to lead me to a source of comfort at the time of his death. These words pointed to the reality of what had just taken place: God had lovingly taken His faithful servant (and my wonderful father) to "heaven, the place of His abode." Dad was being shown the glories of the God he deeply loved, and was finding his joy complete. What comfort I found in this, even in my own time of sorrow. How faithfully God finds ways to speak to us in our times of suffering and how sweet it is to hear His voice. He speaks and the sound of His voice brings comfort.

## THE ENABLING POWER OF COMFORT

God anticipated that grief would be part of the human experience. Throughout Scripture He not only gives us clear assurance of His comfort, but He also urges us to comfort others with that same comfort we have experienced. He has made provision for grief.

Life includes grief because it includes loss. When we talk about comfort and grief and loss, we immediately think in terms of death—the loss of a friend or loved one. But almost all suffering involves loss of some kind, such as the loss of health, finances, employment, or marriage. Each of these can cause tremendous grief because they involve tremendous loss.

The loss of my marriage was a source of deep sorrow for me. I don't think that my husband's death could have caused me any greater grief than the death of our marriage under such awful circumstances. Added to that was the loss of my role as a pastor's wife. I had been called to that role, had been privileged to serve some wonderful churches and people, and had loved that ministry. I mourned the loss of that privilege and responsibility greatly.

Deep and agonizing grief cries out for comfort. Webster's dictionary defines comfort as "to ease the grief or distress of." I hate to argue with Webster, but sometimes it is impossible to ease someone else's grief. Our words, our love, our actions, no matter how well-intentioned and sincere, often aren't enough to diminish the pain of loss.

I would like to suggest another definition—one that comes from my own observations and experiences of grief. I would suggest that comfort is enabling or encouraging someone to go on *in spite of* grief. While our words and loving actions can't always ease someone's grief, they can be the means of enabling that person to simply keep going—to find and take that next step forward. That is a tremendous gift during a time of sorrow and is, I believe, a picture of God's ministry of comfort to us. He comes to us in our grief and enables us to go on.

This comfort is not just a soothing, but a strengthening. "God's comfort is never weakening," wrote Amy Carmichael. "He leaves the soul He comforts stronger to fight, braver to suffer, grateful, not sorry for itself, keen to go on 'to strive, to seek, to find, and not to yield.'"[1] What a clear picture of the enabling power of God's comfort.

In the days following the disclosure of my husband's sin, we purposely withdrew from our church people. We were serving a congregation of about six hundred, and we knew that the love of that many caring people could be overwhelming at that difficult time. So we asked that they give us time to deal with things privately.

Grief was my constant companion as I dealt with the reality and the repercussions of what my husband had done. I woke up to it; I went to bed with it (though not to sleep). It robbed me of the desire to cook or care for my home. I felt a numbness that, oddly enough, didn't release me from the intense suffering I was experiencing. I couldn't express the depth of my pain, even in tears.

God sent His comfort in the form of a man named Walt. Every few days, Walt arrived at our back door, handed me a loaf of homemade raisin bread, said, "I love you," and left. What a simple act! But that simple, loving gesture brought me great comfort. It did nothing to ease the depth of my grief, but that act of kindness did much to enable me to face another day and move forward.

God never tells us not to grieve. In fact, just the opposite is true. He makes it clear in His Word that we will have grief, that it is part of this life, and that all of us will experience it to some degree. He also lets us know that grief is an experience that He understands because it was part of His own life here on earth. That reality alone should bring us comfort.

## A Man of Sorrow

"Jesus wept." How precious are those two words found in John 11:35. Children find that a favorite verse to memorize because of its wonderful brevity. Adults find it a favorite verse to claim because of its wonderful identity—our Savior experienced sorrow and that adds great significance to His comfort.

Grief was such a part of Christ's human experience that Isaiah refers to Him as "a man of sorrows, and acquainted with grief" (Isaiah 53:3 KJV). To many of us these are very familiar words, but we need to let the reality of these words sink into our hearts and minds—to give some deeper thought to their meaning.

To be "of" something indicates "a characteristic or distinctive quality or possession." To be "acquainted" with something implies firsthand knowledge based on personal experience.

Now, let me paraphrase the words of Isaiah 53:3: Christ was a man characterized by sorrow, having firsthand knowledge of grief based on His personal experience. This description of our Savior has great implications for us during our times of grief. The one who is able to give us the greatest comfort during our times of sorrow is someone who can truthfully say, "I understand." (Earlier, we mentioned the impact of those words.) What Isaiah is making clear to us is that, no matter what we face, we have a Savior who comforts us (helps us to go on) with the words, "I understand."

This is expressed again in the familiar words of Hebrews as the writer gives us the qualifications of Jesus as our high priest. "For we have not an high priest which cannot be touched with the feeling of our infirmities" (Hebrews 4:15 KJV). The Greek word that is translated as "feeling" in that verse is *sumpatheo*. Christ is touched with sympathy for us. I find so much comfort in that amazing truth.

Christ understands the feelings or emotions that accompany our suffering. As God, He certainly understands our suffering on a level that we cannot with our finite minds and limited perspective. Yet He was also man, and, as such, Scripture assures us that He also understands the feelings that accompany times of suffering. There is no emotion associated with grief that He hasn't known. That qualifies Him to bring us comfort in our times of sorrow.

In our grief God brings us the comfort of the words "I understand," but He also enables us, through His guidance, to go on. So often in times of great sorrow we are simply at a loss as to what to do next.

## WHAT NEXT?

Sherry and Ken were a vibrant and fun couple in our church. We were stunned when we heard that Ken had been shot in cold blood. A man walked into Ken's office at Syracuse University, pulled a gun, and shot him for no apparent reason. Sherry was left with two small boys and a baby girl, born just a few weeks earlier. After the media attention had worn off and the funeral and public grieving were over, Sherry was left with the huge question, "What next?" Ken was young and had made very few provisions for his death.

I will never forget the assistance that the men of our church gave to her at that time. They helped her figure out financial matters so that she knew what she had to do to take care of her home, her family, and their future. They repaired her porch and her roof. They helped her to go on by giving her practical support and direction.

What a clear picture this is of God's enabling for us during times of sorrow. He is very practical in His help and leading. I discovered this myself during the uncertain days that followed the disclosure of my husband's failures. Sherry's question had become mine—"What next?"

My answer came as I was reading in Joshua. I found tremendous assurance in these wonderful words: "When you see the ark of the covenant of the LORD your God . . . you are to move out from your positions and follow it. *Then you will know which way to go, since you have never been this way before*" (Joshua 3:3–4, emphasis added).

For thirty years I had been joined with my husband in a covenant agreement. The realization that that covenant had been broken left me uncertain and without direction. I had never been this way before! God's assurance was that I was to look to "the ark of the covenant," the ark of His presence. God's presence would go before me on this new and unfamiliar path. He would keep covenant with me and guide my steps. This certainty of His leading for the days ahead, as decisions of great import had to be made, brought me comfort. I faced a new and unfamiliar path, but He would lead the way.

Through the wisdom of His words, God enables us to go

forward in times of grief. We talked in the first chapter about the sweetness of His voice, and in grief that voice becomes a source of great comfort. Over and over again it is His words that give us the strength to go on.

I have just reread my journal from those difficult days and have been filled with awe at the comfort and practical wisdom that God "spoke" to me during that time. Over and over again He gave me Scriptures that brought me help and encouragement. Comfort can never be impersonal, and God's words took on such deep and personal meaning for me during my time of loss.

Just days after my life had changed forever, I read these words: "Though I walk in the midst of trouble, you preserve my life . . . The LORD will fulfill his purpose for me" (Psalm 138:7–8) Then these words from verse 16 of Psalm 139: "All the days ordained for me were written in your book before one of them came to be."

God reminded me that He had known these pages would be written into my life and that nothing was happening that would hinder Him from fulfilling His purpose for my life. What comfort!

## HIS PROMISE AND HIS PRESENCE

Perhaps the greatest source of comfort during the difficult days of grief comes to us through God's promises. David says that he would have never made it without God's promises. In fact, he specifically says that they were his "comfort" (Psalm 119:50). Scripture is full of such promises that give us strength and encouragement.

However, all of these comforts are simply the byproduct of the greatest comfort of all—the promise of God's own presence.

I have just finished re-reading the biography of Keith Green. Keith was a man passionately in love with His Savior who was having tremendous impact through his life and music on the restless youth of the 70s. Then, in a horrific accident, Keith and two of his small children were killed in a plane crash just after take-off from the runway near their ranch in Texas. His wife, Melody, was one of the first people to arrive on the scene. It's hard to imagine her grief as she stared at the burning wreckage and faced the reality of her loss.

She writes: "The only thing that *kept me going* was a sense of the presence of God. I was blanketed in his grace. I felt his presence like I'd never felt it before. Buffering the blows. Holding me. Comforting me. *It didn't ease the pain.* But I felt God's tender heart for me"[2] (emphasis added).

I had written most of this chapter before coming across these words, and I was amazed at how precisely they give validity to the definition that we've been using for comfort. It was God's presence that comforted her and enabled her to keep going. It didn't immediately ease her pain, but it helped her to keep going.

She later states that even more clearly when she says, "The pain was real and constant. When I wanted to lie down and not get up he helped me to my feet."[3] What a clear picture of the comfort that God's presence brings.

It's interesting to note that the original word for comforter in Scripture is *parakletos,* which means "called to one's side." When we grieve, the Holy Comforter himself is called to our side. We are not alone. God himself walks through those dark days with us. That was Melody Green's experience and it was mine also. During my darkest hours I felt God pull me close and gently tuck me under His wing. I grieved tucked up against the Almighty. What comfort!

But it's important to mention something else here. Not everyone who grieves feels God's presence. C. S. Lewis's greatest anguish as he grieved for his wife was the loss of the sense of God's presence. Sometimes we are so numb with grief that we can't feel anything. At other times the pain is so overwhelming that it overshadows all other feelings. The encouragement for us is that God's presence is not based on our feeling but on His promise, and He has promised to walk with us "through the valley of the shadow of death," whatever that death or loss may be (Psalm 23:4). That is His assurance, and He doesn't lie!

Listen to Job's experience as he suffered: "But if I go to the east, he is not there; if I go to the west, I do not find him" (Job 23:8). In the midst of Job's deep grief and tremendous loss, he also lost a sense of the presence of God. But Job was a righteous man who knew God, and he ends with this declaration: "But he knows the way that I take; when he has tested me, I will come forth as gold" (Job 23:10). Job was confident of two things: that God was still aware of him and that his suffering wasn't without purpose. What an amazing testimony under the circumstances!

Christ grieved with Mary and Martha before He raised Lazarus. He shared the sorrow of a widow who had lost her only son and then restored her son to her. We do not have a Savior who is indifferent to our grief, but One who is familiar with it—personally familiar with it.

Include Christ in your grief. Find comfort in His guidance, His wisdom, and, above all, His presence surrounding you and drawing near to you in sorrow. Share Job's confidence and the comfort that confidence can bring: God is with me and He will "bring me forth as gold."

There is no sweetness in grief itself, but there is wonderful sweetness in knowing that God will come alongside us and, through His comfort and care, enable us to go on.

## CHAPTER 7

# The Sweetness of His Names

*Those who know your name will trust in you.*
PSALM 9:10

NAMES ARE IMPORTANT. Before our children are born, we spend months thinking about—sometimes agonizing about—what to name them. We love Aunt Sadie, but do we really want to name our little girl Sadie? If we name our son after one of our twin brothers, will that obligate us to have another boy? (That was my dilemma, but I took the chance and was able to produce the required second son.)

We envision possible nicknames, whether or not the initials will be okay, if the name will sound too grown-up for a child or too childish for a grown-up. We don't want to pick a name that's too old-fashioned, but neither do we want a name that everyone else is choosing.

One of my favorite lines from an old *I Love Lucy* show was when Lucy and Ricky were discussing possible names for their baby. Lucy was adamant that she didn't want the name

John because "every Tom, Dick, and Harry's named John." (I actually know a family where the three sons are named Tom, Dick, and Harry.) Yes, naming a baby can be an arduous task. Perhaps that's why God gives us nine months to work on it!

I have to admit, when I was growing up I hated my name. It wasn't cute, it didn't come with any neat nicknames, and it sounded terribly old-fashioned. Then, a number of years ago, my daughter e-mailed to congratulate me on my name. She said that she had just found out that Esther was in the top ten favorite names for 1998. "Way to go, Mom," she said. "You're finally cool!" However, before I could get over my amazement and respond, a second e-mail followed which brought me quickly back to earth. "Sorry, Mom. Just looked at the list again. It was 1898."

I have learned, however, that there is one advantage to having a name like mine. When I'm in a room and someone calls, "Esther," it's a pretty safe bet that they mean me. Esther! While it certainly wouldn't have been my choice, one thing has made that name special to me. It was a name my father loved, and it was his choice for me.

God the Father also chose the names for His child, and each one has great significance. Centuries before Christ was born, the prophet Isaiah announced God's choice of names for His Son. As he declares in that wonderful and familiar passage, "For to us a child is born, to us a son is given . . . And he will be called Wonderful Counselor, Mighty God, Everlasting Father, Prince of Peace" (Isaiah 9:6). The wonder of these names is that they are not just what the Son of God is called, they're who He is. They are a description of His character and a revelation of His nature. They also point us clearly to His sufficiency for whatever we may be facing.

## A WISE AND WONDERFUL COUNSELOR

First of all, God chose to name His Son *Wonderful Counselor*. One of our greatest needs in a time of suffering is for counsel. Our own judgment is often impaired by our emotions. We are too close to be objective and too weary to be wise. However, human counselors, as helpful as they can be in many instances, are also limited. They don't know the hidden places in our hearts; they don't know the depths of our pain. They only know what we allow them to hear and see.

How comforting to know that God himself is available as our counselor—One who knows our innermost thoughts and feelings, who knows our circumstances, who knows what truly is best, and who knows how it will all end. He assures us, "I will instruct you and teach you in the way you should go; I will counsel you and watch over you" (Psalm 32:8).

Following the initial disclosure of my husband's sins came weeks of proof that any basis for trust was gone. Because of the nature of his sins, I knew that I had clear scriptural "permission" to choose divorce. But it was a time of great heartache for me, and I was afraid of making a decision based on my emotions. I knew that my choice would deeply impact not only my life, but the lives of many that I loved. How could I possibly know what was best? How could I trust my own judgment?

I was encouraged to listen to and accept the counsel of godly people around me—those whom I trusted in their walk with the Lord. However, there was one big problem. Some people that I truly respected and trusted urged me to choose one way, and others that I also knew to be deeply committed Christians felt just as strongly that I should make another choice. Each felt they were right, and each felt strongly that the others were wrong.

In this case, looking to human counsel only led to further confusion. And so I looked to my Wonderful Counselor. As I sought His wisdom, He gently and clearly showed me the way that I should go. When doubts came, He lovingly confirmed His choice and direction through His Word and through specific answers to prayer. I needed that assurance. I needed to be able to look back with certainty and know that I had followed the counsel of the One who can only choose best for me and for all of those who would be affected by my choice. What a comfort that was and what a lifeline for me in the days ahead.

I love that God chose the name Wonderful Counselor for His son. It's a name that gives us hope and encouragement when we are overwhelmed with life. We can bring all of our fears and questions to the One who makes no mistakes—the One who is "wonderful in counsel and magnificent in wisdom" (Isaiah 28:29).

## THE WISDOM OF HIS COUNSEL

When I first met Joyce (not her real name), she appeared to be a rather giggly, carefree young woman. As time went on, it became apparent that the giggles hid a great deal of pain and that her spirit was far from carefree. Her outward demeanor covered a heart bound by the deep hurt and betrayal of sexual abuse.

As I began to counsel her, God (the Wonderful Counselor) gave me the most specific instructions that I had ever been given in a counseling situation. Joyce was basing her life on many of the lies of the Enemy, and God's counsel to me was that as His Spirit revealed those lies for what they were, we would replace them one by one with His truth. This took many months, but over time Joyce began to recognize certain lies that had been the foundation of her life—a rotted, unstable foundation. Slowly, her heart and mind were opened to God's truth.

The first lie was that there was no hope. Joyce was convinced that she would have to live the rest of her life bound by these memories and her hatred of the man who had caused them. God gave us Scripture—His wonderful truth—to demolish that lie, and whenever she would hear that whisper of despair and hopelessness from her enemy, she would declare God's truth.

As one rotten board after another was replaced with God's truth in her life, her foundation became solid and strong—one on which she could stand. The amazing thing is that I discovered that Joyce was actually a deep and thoughtful person, which was a far cry from my first (and false) impression of her.

There is a wonderful PS to Joyce's story that shows us the thoroughness of God's work in our lives as He seeks to counsel us to wholeness. God is not only the Wonderful Counselor, but also the great healer of hearts.

Not long ago, Joyce's grandfather became very ill and was in need of constant care. Joyce was asked by her family to share in this responsibility and become one of his caregivers. What they didn't know, however, was that this was the man who was the source of her pain. It was at his hands that she had suffered the nightmare of sexual abuse as a young girl. As is often the case, the very one who should have been a source of safety and love for her became, instead, a source of horror and fear.

Joyce had spent years carefully avoiding her abuser, not

even wanting to be in the same room with him, and now she was asked to care for this man's body as he lay suffering. Everything in her recoiled at the very thought. After much anguish and prayer, Joyce finally agreed. It wasn't easy to walk into her grandfather's room the first time, but as she did she felt the amazing quiet presence of her heavenly Father and the assurance that this was something He wanted her to do. As the days passed, she began to see her grandfather for what he really was—a damaged, lonely, miserable old man. And slowly she began to realize that God was healing her own wounded spirit.

The Wonderful Counselor had asked a hard thing of her, but He had gently taken her down the very path that would eventually lead to her own restoration. Joyce chose to obey God when He says that we are to "overcome evil with good" (Romans 12:21), and in obedience she found healing for her own wounded heart.

His care is personal, His love is unfailing, His counsel is never wrong. What a perfect name God chose for His Son!

## A Powerful and Mighty Advocate

He also chose the name of Mighty God. I like another version of that name used in Scripture—Almighty God. He's not just mighty, He is all mighty! I like the reminder that His power and might are limitless.

So often in our suffering we face situations for which we truly need an Almighty God. We face problems that are way beyond the scope of human help. We face needs that can't be met by even the most loving friend. We need a powerful and mighty advocate who can do the impossible. We need a Mighty God! For everything for which we need a God, His might and power are sufficient.

A. B. Simpson, a great man of God from the nineteenth century, said that God "is able to do for us all that we need a God for." Suffering makes us keenly aware of that need as it pushes us way beyond our finite limitations. We realize how little might we have as we face the giants of adversity, often feeling overwhelmed and drained. We are not almighty, and we find that there is much that "we need a God for."

I love the story of the man with leprosy who came to Jesus and said, "If you are willing, you can make me clean" (Mark 1:40). There was no question in this man's mind about Christ's power to do the supernatural. He came to Him with absolute confidence and certainty that Jesus could.

We need to come with that same confidence. We need to approach God in prayer with that same declaration as we pray in the name of Jesus, the Almighty God!

Throughout Scripture God clearly reminds us of His power and might. Consider this exchange between the prophet Jeremiah and God. Jeremiah prays, "Ah, Sovereign LORD, you have made the heavens and the earth by your great power and outstretched arm. Nothing is too hard for you" (Jeremiah 32:17). He acknowledges that a look at creation is more than enough evidence that God can do anything. His prayer then goes on to to declare God's might and power, but finishes with some concerns about what God was asking of him personally.

God responds by first stating that He is not only the God of creation, but also the God of all mankind (Jeremiah included). Then He asks, "Is anything too hard for me?" (Jeremiah 32:27). I suspect that was a rhetorical question as God gently reminds Jeremiah of his own words. He is God and nothing is too hard for Him. What a glorious truth!

Valerie's story is one with the fingerprints of the Almighty God all over it. When she and her husband became the proud parents of a healthy baby boy they anticipated the joys of going from being a couple to becoming a family. However, shortly after she gave birth, Valerie's body suddenly shut down. The anxious hours that followed brought little hope. The prognosis was dismal, and the doctors offered little encouragement. They determined that if she survived, her only hope would be a heart transplant. Also, the trauma to her body had destroyed her sight.

Immediately the call went out for prayer, and immediately the family of God responded. Even those of us who didn't know Valerie and Matt personally shared their anguish. I heard of their situation from my son who was their pastor. His heart was broken as he walked through the frightening days with this young couple facing such an uncertain future.

Doctors worked around the clock to find answers and treatments—to no avail. Then the Almighty God stepped in. One day my son went in to see Valerie and found her totally unresponsive as usual. Two days later he returned to find her sitting in a chair, with her husband and newborn baby nearby. (She had not remembered being pregnant so was rather surprised to find out that she had a baby.)

Today as I write this, Valerie continues to improve. Her sight is returning, and the doctors say that her heart has healed and strengthened so that they no longer anticipate the need for a transplant.

This is the work of the Almighty God! I have great respect and admiration for the medical profession. In this day and age amazing things can be done medically, but even modern medicine has its limits. There are times, such as with

Valerie, when there simply aren't human answers or solutions. "But there is a God in heaven," and He bears the name of Almighty!

Let me share another glimpse of the great power of God in a setting that is worlds apart from a hospital room in upstate New York. It takes place in the Middle East, in a city physically and emotionally crippled by years of war and terrorism. There among the devastation and destruction stands a building with a sign above it boldly declaring that "Jesus is the Light of the World."

The church housed in that building is large and growing in spite of the constant threats against its people. It has become a place of quiet in the midst of chaos, a place of peace in the midst of war. Many have found eternal answers in a world with no easy temporal answers.

I remember the day that we got the news that the youth pastor of this church had been kidnapped by terrorists and was being held for ransom. Knowing the nature of these terrorists gave little reason for hope. Killing was their sport and their mission. Even if the church had been able to raise the amount of money that was being demanded, it was still no guarantee of the release of their pastor.

"But there is a God in heaven," and it was to Him that this church, and the church worldwide, turned in this time of urgent need. We joined our hearts with his young wife and children as we beseeched the Almighty on behalf of this faithful servant of God.

God did what man could not. For "some unknown reason," the terrorists decided to release Ahmed (not his real name). He was unbound and taken to a room where he was told to find his ID tag and leave. The bag in which he had to search for his

ID was a large garbage bag filled with the ID tags of those who had already been brutally killed. There is no explanation for his release other than the mighty power of God.

What a wonderful name God chose for His Son who continues to display the wonder of that name on behalf of a young family in New York and against the powers of darkness in Baghdad. He is still the Mighty God!

## A FOREVER FATHER

The next name given to Jesus is one that is especially meaningful to me. Imagine a child—a baby—being given the name Everlasting Father. But through this name God was communicating the amazing truth that this child would not just be His Son and bear His name; He would also be Him in all His fullness. This was not to be a miniature God or a copy of God; this baby would be "in very nature God" (Philippians 2:6), and God's nature and heart is that of an Everlasting Father.

For me this name has great significance because of my earthly father. I have always found great comfort in coming to God as my Father because I was always sure of the love and acceptance of the man I called "Daddy."

My father was a busy pastor, but occasionally he would have time to sit down for a few minutes and read the paper. That meant I couldn't see his face, so I would crawl up between his crossed legs and put my chubby little face right between him and the paper.

Looking back, I realize how much he probably looked forward to and needed those few quiet minutes to sit and read. However, I was always lovingly welcomed and invited to sit on his lap and snuggle down.

Those who know me also know that I probably didn't just sit there quietly and let the poor man get back to his reading. I'm sure that I had much on my young mind that I felt he would certainly want to hear. As a result, I am very comfortable approaching my heavenly Father with all that's on my mind. There is nothing too small, but even more wonderful, there is nothing too big.

Some of you, however, have painful memories associated with the name "father." For some of you, that very name adds to your suffering. But for you there is the hope that all that you failed to find in your earthly father—and much more—is available for you in the One named "the Everlasting Father."

I brought to my earthly father all my hurts, all my broken things, all my fears and problems with the confidence that he loved me and that I had every right to come to him. There is One waiting with open arms who will always welcome you as my father welcomed me. He will not fail you. He will not push you away. He will listen and love and care and provide. And He can heal and comfort with more love than any of us can fathom.

My father was an amazing father, but he was a mere shadow of the Everlasting Father. Come in prayer with that same confidence that I had as I sought my father's face behind his paper. Find the face of your eternal Father as you come to Him in confidence in the wonderful name of His own Son.

## A Source of Peace that Guides and Guards

Suffering does not produce peace. Our times of heartache and pain produce many emotions, but peace is not one of them. We may experience gripping fear, overwhelming discouragement, bitter anger, or deep grief. All of these negate peace.

Peace is not a natural by-product of suffering. It can be, however, a supernatural by-product because of the One named the Prince of Peace, the final name given prophetically to Christ in Isaiah 9:6.

How can you find peace when everything around you is falling apart, when all of your life is in turmoil, when you are in the midst of pain? The answer to each of these is the same. We can only find peace through finding its source—the wonderful Prince of Peace.

When I was a child, I listened to a missionary tell about crossing a rope bridge over a deep ravine in Indonesia. Underneath her were swirling waters and rocks. One missed step meant certain death. Her only hope was to hang on and walk forward—each step more frightening than the last.

Ahead of her was her guide, and as they moved forward inch by inch he spoke these words to her: "Don't look down. Just look at me. Keep your eyes on me and put your feet where I put mine." As she took her focus off the flimsy bridge, the dizzying height, and the rocky waters below, she experienced a calm that surprised her. As long as she looked at her guide and followed in his steps she could overcome the panic and fear that gripped her.

The lesson is obvious. Our only hope for that "peace that passes understanding" is to keep our eyes on our Guide and to put our feet in His footsteps.

One of my closest friends has recently faced something as uncertain and frightening as that rope bridge. Some weeks ago both of Kathy's parents disappeared. Under the best of circumstances that is horrifying news, but Kathy's parents aren't in the best of circumstances. Kathy's mother has diabetes, and they both suffer from Alzheimer's. As is sometimes typical of people with Alzheimer's, Kathy's mother is given to bouts of rage. In one of those moments she pushed their caregiver out of the car, grabbed the keys, and took off with Kathy's father. There has been an intense search covering three states with much media coverage in an attempt to find them. During these weeks Kathy has dealt with the many emotions normal at a time like this. But I can honestly say that the predominate emotion that is evident in Kathy as she walks through these frightening days is one of peace. She is not looking down, but keeping her eyes focused on her Guide over these very troubled waters.

Two pictures of peace in Scripture have helped me many times. First, Paul urges the believers at Colosse to "Let the peace of Christ rule in your hearts" (Colossians 3:15). Then he assures the Christians at Philippi that "the peace of God, which transcends all understanding, will guard your hearts and your minds in Christ Jesus" (Philippians 4:7).

In the first picture, Paul encourages us to let God's peace rule in every circumstance, to let His peace be sovereign over all the other emotions. That's what Kathy is doing. She is feeling the pull of many emotions—fear, worry, panic—but she is allowing God's peace to be the emotion that rules over her heart. Peace must have the victory because it is from God!

But peace cannot rule unless the Prince of Peace rules. If there are areas in your life that are not yielded to the sovereignty of God, you will not find peace. If there is rebellion or disobedience, peace cannot rule. God administers peace in hearts and minds over which He administers control. Paul puts it like this: "The mind controlled by the Spirit is life and peace" (Romans 8:6).

The second picture is that of peace standing guard at the

door of our hearts and minds. Those fearful thoughts, those bitter, angry feelings, are stopped at the entrance by peace. Notice two important things that Paul mentions about this peace. First, it "transcends all understanding." There is nothing logical about it. It is offered to us when it is the most illogical of all emotions to have at that time. Second, it is found "in Christ Jesus." We can't conjure this up or will it into being. There is a source, and it is the Prince of Peace himself.

When actress Patty Duke was rehearsing for the role of Helen Keller on Broadway, she disciplined herself to be oblivious to the sights and sounds going on around her so that she could identify more with the world of the blind and deaf Helen Keller. She had to work hard to tune out all the noises and to ignore all the visible things happening around her on stage. She had to attempt to become "blind and deaf" to them.

One day there was an accident on the set when some sandbags dropped to the stage from high overhead. Everyone ran and screamed. Everyone except Patty Duke. She quietly remained as she was, unaffected by the confusion around her.

What a picture of what God offers us as the Prince of Peace. He offers us a "peace that passes understanding"—a peace that can remain quiet even when sandbags fall around us. Patty Duke had done her best to enter another world—the silent, sightless world of Helen Keller. We too are to be of another world—a world where the sights and sounds around us are quieted by the presence of God's wonderful peace.

## THE POWER OF HIS NAMES

When God taught me this wonderful lesson about these (and other) names of Christ, I began thinking about what it means to pray "in Jesus name." We are instructed to pray in His name, but it is so much more than just tacking an "in Jesus' name" at the end of our prayer. My only access to God is through the One who bears the names of Wonderful Counselor, Mighty God, Everlasting Father, and Prince of Peace. This added such a rich dimension to my prayers and a new understanding of the significance of praying in His name(s).

We pray in the name of the Wonderful Counselor. We bring our needs to one bearing the name of Almighty (all mighty) God. We ask of one who is our Everlasting Abba Father. And we come in our times of turmoil to one who is the Prince of Peace.

Think of how meaningful each of those names is for our times of suffering. But even more, think of how meaningful all of those names are together. I love the wholeness of our God, who gave His Son each of those names so that together they would show us a picture of His glorious sufficiency.

Imagine if He were a loving father with no wisdom. Or what if He were loving and wise, but had no power to accomplish what His love desired and His wisdom knew to be best. We can rest in His peace because we know that He is all wise, all loving, and all mighty. What a perfect God!

What a difference it makes in prayer as we come to the Father in these names that He chose for His own Son. And we find that there is a sweetness in these names that ministers to us at the deepest point of our need.

## CHAPTER 8

# The Sweetness of His Grace

*I pray that out of his glorious riches he may strengthen you*
*with power through his Spirit in your inner being.*

EPHESIANS 3:16

GRACE IS A wonderful thing to experience, but a difficult thing to define. Jim Cymbala expresses it like this: "*Grace* is a rich and multifaceted word in the New Testament. One of its primary meanings is God doing for us, by the Holy Spirit, what we cannot do for ourselves."[1] And, I would add, what we don't deserve for Him to do. Grace always implies something not merited.

Others have described grace as "God's Righteousness at Christ's Expense" or "God's Riches at Christ's Expense." These are more than just a clever play on words, for they do give us some insight into the nature of grace. But they still leave us without a concise and clear understanding of its full meaning and measure.

One hymn writer chose to use "amazing" as the adjective for grace. The appropriateness of that adjective is made clear in the words that follow.

*Amazing grace! How sweet the sound*
*That saved a wretch like me!*
*I once was lost, but now am found,*
*Was blind, but now I see.*

*T'was grace that taught my heart to fear,*
*And grace my fears relieved;*
*How precious did that grace appear*
*The hour I first believed!*

*Through many dangers, toils and snares,*
*I have already come;*
*'Tis grace hath brought me safe thus far,*
*And grace will lead me home.*

Grace offers salvation to the worst of sinners; it finds the lost and brings sight to the spiritually blind. Grace reveals the frightening condition of our hearts, and then puts our fears to rest. And it is that same grace that brings us safely through the "dangers, toils and snares" that threaten us in this life.

The author of these words was John Newton, who spent many years of his life engaged in the evils of the slave trade. He found his salvation a continual source of wonder, and these words came from the overflow of his heart in testimony to God's amazing grace. No wonder he found those words to have a sweet sound.

Grace *is* amazing because it offers us all that we need for this present life. It is God's abundance made available to us through the suffering and death of His own Son. And the final triumph of this amazing grace will be to bring us safely home into the eternal presence of our awesome and holy God.

## A Room Full of Grace

Even as I write these words I am frustrated by my inability to express this truth in a way that leaves us with hearts that are overwhelmed with love and gratitude. Words are inadequate to fully express grace because grace is greater than any definition.

There is an illustration in Scripture, however, that has been a tremendous help to me in understanding the impact of grace in my life, especially in those times of "dangers, toils and snares."

In 2 Chronicles 5:1 we find these words: "When all the work Solomon had done for the temple of the LORD was finished, he brought in the things his father David had dedicated—the silver and gold and all the furnishings—and he placed them in the treasuries of God's temple." Notice that Solomon didn't bring anything of his own. His father, King David, had already made provision for him.

What gives these words special meaning for me is that Paul, in the New Testament, reminds us emphatically that we are now the temple of God: "Don't you know that you yourselves are God's temple and that God's Spirit lives in you?" (1 Corinthians 3:16). "For we are the temple of the living God" (2 Corinthians 6:16). Solomon's great structure has been replaced with living temples—that's us—that house the very presence of the Almighty. So if Solomon's temple had treasuries supplied by his father, is it a far stretch to believe that we, as God's temple, also have treasuries from our Father—places where all of our Father's riches are stored for our use? Grace truly is "God's riches at Christ's expense," and those riches are available to us.

This realization has become very practical for me in my times of suffering. As I face situations for which I am inadequate, I am aware that God has an ample supply of all that I need for that moment. When we think He has given us more than we can bear, we have only to look at the riches provided through His abundant grace.

For years I thought of myself as God's temple in terms of being a place of sacrifice. My heart was an altar, and it was there that I surrendered my will and my wishes to His. It was at the temple altar that I would lay my self and its pride to be put to death. But for many years I missed out on the joy of knowing that my temple was also a place with storerooms filled with God's abundant supply.

Peter expresses this same thought when he assures us that God's "divine power has given us everything we need for life and godliness" (2 Peter 1:3). It is not by accident or exaggeration that Peter uses the word *everything*. Nor is it wishful thinking to believe that that word applies to both the temporal needs of this life and the eternal needs of our heart. God has His own limitless supplies stored in the treasuries of our heart to be drawn out and used when our own resources run dry.

This is grace! And the joy comes with the realization that what can't be fully expressed in words can be fully experienced in our times of suffering.

Grace is like being given someone else's credit card for all of our needs. All of our expenses have been paid in advance (at great cost) and our credit line is unlimited. That means, in practical terms, that the greatness of our suffering and needs will never surpass the abundance of God's supply. Like the manna in the wilderness, the supply is always adequate for the needs of the day.

It is grace that allowed Betsie ten Boom to declare in the midst of the horrors of the Nazi concentration camp, "There is no pit so deep that He is not deeper still!" She had learned, even in that dark and evil place, the secret of drawing from the treasuries of her heart all she needed to face the fears and suffering of each new day. No enemy could rob her of that rich store of God's provision.

When suffering makes us keenly aware of our own limitations, it is such a blessing to know that we can find within our own hearts a rich supply of "God's riches" purchased for us "at Christ's expense."

## A RICH SUPPLY OF TRUST

While our treasuries truly contain all that each of us needs, I would like to look at a few specific things that we find stored there for our use. Taped on the shelf above my desk are these words from Jim Cymbala, "The hardest part of faith is often simply to wait." I would expand that to say that the hardest part of suffering is often to wait: to wait for test results, to wait for answers, to wait to be free of pain, to wait for a marriage to be restored, to wait for a job or financial relief, to wait for a wayward child to come home . . . and the list goes on and on.

When suffering seems endless and we find ourselves weary of waiting, God's grace opens the door of our treasuries and shows us a rich supply of trust that allows us to patiently wait.

God's timing is often different from ours. In this regard, a verse that I love and have clung to many times is Isaiah 60:22: "I am the LORD; in its time I will do this swiftly."

What a great reminder that God will not delay, nor will He be rushed. While we are wearily waiting, He is working in ways we can't see or know. So our trust is based on God's own assurance that when the time is right, He won't make us wait any longer. We have no choice about waiting, but we do have a choice about whether we will draw from God's supply of trust so that we can wait with a patient, quiet heart for Him to work in His time and His way.

## FORGIVENESS BEYOND OUR OWN

Another supply that God has put in our treasuries is the grace of forgiveness. Sometimes our suffering is the result of someone else's choices or sin. We find ourselves unable to forgive because the wrong has been so great or has had such devastating results in our lives. I have counseled so many women who have simply said of forgiveness, "I can't!" And often, we can't!

One woman in particular had been deeply hurt by her mother during her childhood years. Now, as an adult, she suffered from panic attacks and anorexia, among other emotional disorders. She sat across the table from me and said, "Don't even ask me to forgive my mother. I can't and I won't." It broke my heart to see her turn her back on God's path to her own healing. Her hurts were slowly destroying her because she refused to avail herself of God's rich supply of grace.

God offers us enough forgiveness to cover the deepest hurt. A powerful example of this is found in the life of Corrie ten Boom. She saw evil up close and personal as, day after day, she and countless others suffered at the hands of the Nazi prison guards. She looked into eyes that never showed a trace of kindness or mercy toward those who were suffering under their cruel tyranny. A number of years after Corrie's release, she was back in Germany, this time to speak words of healing and encouragement to the German people. At the close of one service she suddenly found herself looking into the eyes of one of her captors. Immediately her mind flashed back to the humiliation and shame she and Betsie had suffered at the hands of this man. Now he stood in front of her with his hand outstretched, asking for her forgiveness. She had none to offer, but listen to her own words as she describes how she drew from the treasury of grace that God had placed within her heart.

"I tried to smile, I struggled to raise my hand. I could not. I felt nothing, not the slightest spark of warmth or charity. And so . . . I breathed a silent prayer. *Jesus, I cannot forgive him. Give me Your forgiveness.*

"As I took his hand the most incredible thing happened. From my shoulder along my arm and through my hand a current seemed to pass from me to him, while into my heart sprang a love for this stranger that almost overwhelmed me."[2]

What Corrie experienced is expressed best by Oswald Chambers' definition of grace: "'Grace' means the overflowing nature of God."[3] It was God's nature that flowed through Corrie in that moment and allowed her to offer what she didn't have in herself to give. What an incredible truth! It is God's own nature that we find stored up for us in abundance in the treasuries of our temple.

Peter shares this same thought right after he assures us that God makes available to us all that we need for life and godliness. He then gives us the secret of this abundant supply. It is because God allows us the amazing privilege to "participate in the divine nature" (2 Peter 1:4).

The actual unlimited resources of God's own divine nature are available to us in our time of need, when our own resources have run dry, in our weariness and anguish, in the deepest night of suffering.

I get so excited as I write these words. This grace, this supply of God's great riches, is available in the treasuries of each of our hearts as children of God. We have God's own attributes, His own divine nature, to draw from when we have no resources of our own. Truly, what amazing grace!

## A Cache of Courage

When Peter and I were struggling to keep our business afloat, it was a time of great fear for me. Would we be able to pay our workers this week? Would a check arrive in time for us to have Christmas presents for the kids? What would happen if the business failed? Would we lose our home? Morning after morning I would wake up with the cold hand of fear gripping my heart. As a writer I know the importance of avoiding overused expressions and clichés such as "the cold hand of fear," but that is exactly how it felt. And this brings us to one more treasure that is ours for the taking at our time of need.

Over and over again in Scripture we read, "Do not be afraid." God spoke these words to Abram at the time of the covenant, to Hagar as she fled with her young son from the displeasure of her mistress Sarah, to Joshua as he took over the responsibility of leading the children of Israel, to the nation of Israel as they faced enemies that were larger and more powerful, and to Mary and Joseph as they received the startling news of their role in the birth of God's Son, Jesus.

Each time these words were spoken there was a very real reason for fear. And each time these words were spoken, God gave a very real reason not to fear. He promised Abram that He would be his shield. He assured Hagar that He heard the cry of her son. He promised His presence to Joshua, His power to the nation of Israel, and assured Mary and Joseph that what was about to happen was His perfect plan.

In reading back over my journals I am amazed at how many times I cried out to God in fear. Each time there was a very real reason for me to fear. And each time God gave me a very real reason not to fear. Over and over again He met my fear with assurance, not a reprimand. He didn't always take away the fearful circumstances, but He always brought His own presence and promises into those frightening situations. It was at one of those times that I wrote these words to express my experience of God's gracious help.

*Frightening are the waves about me*
*Hidden is the shore,*
*Nothing solid underneath me*
*Sinking evermore.*

*I had left the boat behind me*
*Bravely stepping out,*
*But I now was slowly sinking*
*Drowning in my doubt.*

*Then I felt a hand reach toward me*
*Felt His hold on me,*

*And together we went forward*
*Dancing on the sea!*

There are many reasons for fear, but none of them stand up against the reasons not to fear. God has a treasury full of promises that bring us courage as we face fearful circumstances, and none is greater than the promise of His own presence. He still says, "It is I; don't be afraid." (John 6:20)

Think of the significance and power of those simple words, "It is I." It is I, the Almighty God; it is I, the Sovereign King; it is I, the Great Shepherd; it is I, the Rock, the Fortress, the Deliverer, the Healer, the Comforter. It is I, the Great I AM!

Fear cannot stand in the presence of God. What amazing grace!

## BE ON GUARD!

These are just a few of the great riches made available to us by God's amazing grace. If we were to examine all the wealth God has placed at our disposal, this chapter could easily evolve into a book of its own.

I grew up in a denomination where I frequently heard the phrase "the all-sufficiency of Christ." That is a beautiful and accurate summary of the vast riches stored for us in the treasuries of our hearts. We overflow with all that we need through His wonderful grace.

But there is one last truth that needs to be considered as we focus on the sweetness of God's grace. And here we draw again from a clear lesson that we find in Scripture. Listen to this tragic account found in 2 Chronicles 12:9: "When Shishak king of Egypt attacked Jerusalem, he carried off the treasures of the temple of the LORD."

This is a sad and often repeated part of Israel's history. Invading armies would conquer the nation of Israel and then carry off the treasures from the temple of God. One of Jeremiah's laments after the destruction of the temple and the exile of the Jews to Babylon was this: "The enemy laid hands on all her treasures" (Lamentations 1:10).

What a tragic part of Israel's history, but what a clear warning for us today! We also have an enemy who wants to invade our lives at times of weakness and steal our treasures. How often have you experienced Satan's whispers and lies that rob you of hope and peace, of joy and patience? Satan's desire is to empty out of our treasuries all that grace has put in.

Israel had one primary purpose: to reveal the reality and power of their God to the nations that surrounded them. A big part of that revelation was to come through their victories over their enemies, who were usually stronger and more adequately equipped for battle. What an opportunity for God to display His greatness and power for all to see!

So it is with men and women of faith. We are called to bear witness to the reality of a living, mighty God to those around us. And suffering affords us a unique opportunity to display this as we respond in victory to the powerful foes and battles we face. There is no greater witness for Christ than a Christian who is triumphant in suffering.

Satan will do anything to rob us of that opportunity. He cannot bear to see God lifted up as victor, and so he tries to take from us all that is rightfully ours. He comes to carry off the treasures that God has placed in us, His holy temple—all that we need for life and godliness, all the riches that have their source in His own divine nature. We must jealously guard this wealth from the lies and attacks of the Enemy and joyously claim all that God has placed there for our use and His glory.

"Amazing grace" the songwriter declared, and our hearts echo that song. God has filled our treasuries so that we don't ever need to depend on our own limited supplies. He has enough for whatever we face and gives it freely and in abundance, and that is truly the sweetness of His wonderful and marvelous grace.

## Chapter 9

# The Sweetness of His Correction

*The Lord disciplines those he loves.*
PROVERBS 3:12

THERE WAS ALWAYS a sense of relief when all three of my young children were finally tucked into bed at night and things were quiet. Often the quiet didn't last long, and this particular night was no exception. I soon heard the voice of my young daughter calling for me. I chose to ignore it at first, but soon heard it again—a little more emphatically: "Mommy!" I pulled my weary bones up from the couch and went to her room.

Debbie was genuinely troubled and shared that she wanted Jesus to come into her heart. I gently questioned her to make sure she understood the importance of this step she was taking, and then we prayed. What a precious interruption!

At that point, her father came to the door and, not realizing what had just happened, said in a rather stern voice, "Debbie, if your mother has to come in here again, you'll have to be punished." As we turned out the light to leave, we heard the rather indignant voice of our little new believer say, "Well, you don't punish Christians, you know!"

Not only do we occasionally have to punish the little Christians that we have in our homes, but God's deep love for us also includes His hand of correction. It is impossible to write about suffering without recognizing the possibility of it being a means for God to correct or discipline us.

## THE BENEFITS OF CORRECTION

I have to be honest. I have never received or given discipline where my reaction was, "Well, wasn't that sweet?" No, the sweetness is not found in the correction; it's found in the love that prompts it and the results that justify it.

Discipline has a purpose. When administered correctly it is never to relieve the frustration or anger of the parent, but to assure a change in the attitude or behavior of the child for the child's sake. Scripture goes so far as to say that an undisciplined child is like an illegitimate child. God proves that we are His by His loving correction.

We discipline our children because we have a specific goal and purpose for them. We want them to become responsible adults. We hope that they will become people of character and integrity, and our goal is to "refine" them from all that is contrary to that.

One of my goals as a parent was to raise my children to be adults who didn't whine and complain about their responsibilities. In pursuit of that goal, I learned early on that talking had little effect, but consequences usually brought much faster results. So if I gave them a job to do and they whined or complained, they were instantly given another one. It didn't take them long to realize that to complain was self-defeating. And while I can't say that they did all of their chores cheerfully, they usually didn't do a lot of grumbling.

God also has a goal in raising His children, and it's made clear in Scripture. Ephesians 1:4 states: "For he chose us in him before the creation of the world to be holy and blameless in his sight."

We know very little about God prior to creation. It is in the creation story that we are first introduced to the Godhead and begin to learn of His power and greatness. However, in this verse we get a peek into the heart of God before creation, and we find that even before we existed He chose for us to be "holy and blameless in his sight." He has a specific parenting goal, and sometimes it takes His loving correction to get us there.

Scripture never actually calls correction sweet, but it does come pretty close when the psalmist declares, "Blessed is the man you discipline, O LORD" (Psalm 94:12). *The Amplified Bible* puts it this way: "Blessed (happy, fortunate, to be envied) is the man whom You discipline and instruct, O Lord."

God's discipline is proof of His personal awareness of us, His love and concern for us, and His loving involvement in our lives. That is so humbling and amazing. The God of the universe, King of Kings, Almighty Creator, the Holy God cares enough about me to know when I need His hand applied in loving correction, and nothing will dissuade Him from following through. He loves us too much to let our need for correction slide.

## DISCIPLINE AND PUNISHMENT ARE NOT THE SAME

It's important at this point to make the distinction between discipline or correction and punishment. Correction is exactly that—its purpose is to correct, to make right and bring about changes, whether in behavior or attitude. Punishment is necessary when correction has been ineffective or ignored, when there has been direct defiance of established rules.

We see this repeatedly in the story of God's relationship with the nation of Israel. He would discipline them over and over again, and finally, when they had not repented and responded to His correction, He would have to punish them. In His love and mercy He would offer them opportunity after opportunity to submit to His correction; when all else failed, He would use punishment to bring about correction.

One of the powerful images God uses to depict His work of discipline and correction in His people is the refiner's fire. For example, this passage in Isaiah 1:25–26:

> *I will turn my hand against you;*
> *I will thoroughly purge away your dross*
> *and remove all your impurities.*
> *I will restore your judges as in days of old,*
> *your counselors as at the beginning.*
> *Afterward you will be called*
> *the City of Righteousness,*
> *the Faithful City.*

The prophet begins with the warning to Israel that God "will turn His hand against them." After the warning, God then explains His purpose: "I will thoroughly purge away your dross and remove all your impurities." In other words, I will refine you. That's not a pleasant process, but look at the next words: "I will restore . . ." God has a purpose in this correction. He desires their restoration as His people.

He then lets them know the end results: "Afterward you will be called the City of Righteousness, the Faithful City." He is letting them know that there's a sweet side to all of this!

If we read the following verses, we see the frightening contrast of punishment. This is God's warning of what will happen to "rebels and sinners"—those who do not respond to His restorative process of correction and discipline. These will "be broken, and those who forsake the Lord will perish." This is punishment. All of God's correction—His refiner's fire—even when it's painful, is intended to spare us from punishment.

It is important to make one thing clear: I do not believe that all suffering is God's punishment.

When I was in my early twenties, I had most of my stomach removed due to a gastric ulcer. My husband was in seminary at the time, and as a result, I was at the receiving end of the various theological views that run rampant in that environment. One, however, stands out in my mind. According to one young seminarian, there was only one possible explanation for my suffering. I had sinned, and God was punishing me. I remember the emotional and spiritual pain I experienced as he handed down that judgment.

And so, while I would never lump all suffering as punishment from God, I do believe that occasionally suffering can be the Lord's loving and restorative correction. But the sweetness is there—even in this.

In one time of suffering God led me to the old hymn "How Firm a Foundation." I was almost annoyed at His choice. How could this quaint hymn minister to my present need? Then I read the words—wonderful, meaningful words! I had sung that hymn all my life without really listening to the words. That night I did, and they brought me an understanding of my present struggle with pain—a perspective based on the truth of God's Word.

This hymn conveys solid, scriptural truth that can give meaning to what appears to be meaningless suffering.

> *"When through fiery trials thy pathway shall lie,*
> *My grace, all sufficient, shall be thy supply:*
> *The flame shall not hurt thee; I only design*
> *Thy dross to consume, and thy gold to refine."*

Our suffering is not meaningless! God will use the painful fire of suffering to purify us and has assured us of His all-sufficient grace as we face the flames.

## PURITY'S PAINFUL PROCESS

Let's look further at the illustration of the refiner's fire. What is being refined? In using the image of God as the refiner, the prophet Malachi declares: "He will sit as a refiner and purifier of silver; he will purify . . . and refine them like gold and silver" (3:3). And the Isaiah passage we have referred to says, "Your silver has become dross" (1:22).

What is being refined is silver or gold—something of great worth. Please hear this: The refiner only invests his time and effort in something of value. There was a saying that was popular a few years ago that was rather crude, but makes an important point: "God don't make no junk." We could rephrase that to say, "God don't refine no tin."

We need no further proof of God's opinion of our worth than the cross. It is a profound display of love that has no limits and only seeks a response from us. It is a love that is unfailing and eternal and intensely personal.

And it is this Love that holds us in His hands and places us in the crucible to be refined. We are not held in uncaring hands. The One who holds us finds no joy in subjecting us to the fire, only in the end result. Job understood this when he said, "When He has tried me, I shall come forth as refined gold (pure and luminous)" (Job 23:10 AB). Pure and luminous, holy and blameless is what He has always desired us to be—even "before the creation of the world."

And what is it that purifies gold? It is fire. Gold can't be purified from the dross within by polishing the outside. It takes a breaking down of the basic structure of the gold to allow all that is impure to be burned away, and it is fire that accomplishes this.

There is a wonderful story told by Amy Carmichael. One day she took a group of Indian children to see a goldsmith. They watched as he held the gold in the fire. He then removed it, studied it carefully, turned up the flame, and put the gold into the fire again.

After watching this process for some time, Amy asked, "When do you know it is pure?"

"When I can see my face in it," he said.[1]

What a picture of our divine Refiner. He desires our purity above our comfort so that His face can be accurately reflected in us. We recoil from the flame, but we need to fear the lack of purity more than we fear the flame. After all, His only design is "our dross to consume and our gold to refine."

Another illustration of this process is much more familiar

to our twenty-first century lives. It's the process of chemo-therapy or radiation to eliminate cancer.

My cousin's vivacious little six-year-old is going through a radical treatment to fight a particularly aggressive and inva-sive form of cancer. Why put a little girl through the dis-comfort of chemotherapy? Why allow her to suffer the often agonizing side effects? Why not put a stop to it when her long, curly hair begins to fall out? Why? The answer is obvious. Her parents love her so much that they are willing to subject her to whatever is necessary to rid her of the cancer that has invaded her precious little body.

Can you imagine a doctor telling a cancer patient that all she needs to do is go out and get a new hairstyle, a make-over, and a new wardrobe, and she'll be fine. All that can do is make her look good on the outside; it does nothing to eradicate the impurities inside. A new "look" just won't do it. It requires the "fire" of chemotherapy or radiation.

So it is with our Refiner. He won't allow us to polish ourselves up into nice-looking Christians outwardly while ignoring the impurity within. It's His love that holds us in the fire.

## THE PAY-OFF OF PAIN

My life is a huge "Amen" to the work that suffering can do. I didn't realize all the dross or impurities that were in me. I was oblivious to hidden areas of pride and self-righteousness. God used suffering to humble me and to cleanse me. The fire was difficult and painful and sometimes seemed endless. But I am so thankful for the love of my Refiner who continued to return me to the flame.

What a shame to be robbed of the benefits of suffering.

We can come to the end of our times of suffering having experienced nothing but the suffering, or we can allow the Lord to do the work He desires to do—to squeeze every possible benefit and good that can come from it. We can ask Him to do His work of loving correction in our lives to create something of great value—pure gold.

The writer of Hebrews gives us a glimpse of the gold that comes from refining: "God disciplines us for our good, that we may share in his holiness" (Hebrews 12:10). I wish that I could write those words in neon lights. I wish that we could grasp the value of our temporal suffering, no matter how intense, in light of that eternal reward.

Andrew Murray says this in reference to Hebrews 12:10: "Of all the precious words Holy Scripture has for the sorrowful, there is hardly one equal to this in leading us more directly and more deeply into the fullness of blessing that suffering is meant to bring. It is His holiness, God's own holiness, of which we are to partake."[2] What can be sweeter than that?

These words in Hebrews give us hope for now—for the present. They offer us the promise that the end result is the holiness of God himself manifest in our lives. Paul adds to that truth by reminding us of what's ahead. He makes it clear that the suffering we experience now can't even be compared to the glory ahead: "I consider that our present sufferings are not worth comparing with the glory that will be revealed in us" (Romans 8:18).

No, suffering is not sweet; it's not even pleasant. The refining fire is still fire. But when we know that it's our loving Father's hand that holds us there, we can know that it will not be wasted. He is creating out of us a gold that will allow

His face to be seen. We become what He planned for us to be before the beginning of time. It is one of suffering's sweetest rewards.

## CHAPTER 10

# The Sweetness of Hope

*"Those who hope in me will not be disappointed."*
ISAIAH 49:23

"SO STRONG, SO BEAUTIFUL is hope that it is scarcely possible to overpraise it," wrote A. W. Tozer. "It is the divine alchemy that transmutes the base metal of adversity into gold."[1] Simply put, hope is one of the sweet sides of adversity or suffering.

It is hard to adequately express the importance of hope. Hope has given people the courage to face insurmountable odds, to accomplish great feats of heroism, and sometimes just to put one foot in front of the other.

Dr. Jerome Groopman, the author of *The Anatomy of Hope,* says this: "We are just beginning to appreciate hope's reach and have not defined its limits.[2] Hope is one of our central emotions, but we are often at a loss when asked to define it. Many of us confuse hope with optimism." But, he says, "Hope, unlike optimism, is rooted in unalloyed reality."[3]

The dictionary defines hope as the ability "to cherish a desire with anticipation," although we often use the word to mean far less than that. We respond to someone's words of encouragement with, "I hope so." What that means is that I have no solid confidence or assurance, but that with any luck it will happen the way I desire.

The hope put forth in Scripture is much more in keeping with Groopman's definition than with Webster's. It is a claim, an assurance of something not yet realized, but unquestioningly certain. Hope is not crossed fingers, but a settled heart.

## LOST HOPE

The role that hope plays in our times of suffering is difficult to measure. But we do know that to lose hope in the midst of suffering is devastating.

I saw this vividly displayed as I recently watched a DVD of the Brooklyn Tabernacle Singers in concert at Angola, a high-security state penitentiary in Louisiana for those serving life sentences and those awaiting execution.

As many of the prisoners shared their amazing testimonies, I was struck by one sentiment that was voiced again and again by these men. Almost without exception they said that they had experienced an overwhelming sense of hopelessness when the prison doors first locked behind them and they faced the awful realization that there was no longer any life for them apart from the confines of the cement block walls of Angola. Many of them contemplated suicide as the only remedy for a life without hope. Only through God's saving grace was their hope restored!

To be robbed of hope is one of life's most devastating and crippling experiences. In chapter 5, I wrote about the tragic plane crash in the Andes Mountains in 1972. Among the survivors was a young man named Marcelo who instantly became the leader and encourager of them all. "Much of the credit for our survival in those critical early days must go to Marcelo Perez," says Nando Parrado in *Miracle in the Andes*.[4] He organized the rescue efforts, took steps to provide what little shelter their surroundings could afford them, but most of all he gave them hope. "More than anything, he buoyed our spirits by convincing us that our suffering would soon be over."[5]

Over the days that followed, Marcelo continued to display that quality. He continually encouraged the others not to give up, assuring them that they would be rescued. Many of them owed their lives to the hope that Marcelo instilled in them.

Among the things the survivors found in the wreckage of the plane was a battery-operated transistor radio. One of the young men was able to rig up a make-shift antenna that offered occasional and very limited reception. On the morning of their eleventh day on the mountain, just as they were about to turn the radio off, the survivors heard a news report. What they heard was as chilling as the mountain air around them. The search for them had been called off. The reporter said that in addition to the dangers of continuing the search, it was believed that after this many days there could be no survivors. The rescuers had given up hope.

The impact of that news was staggering, especially for Marcelo. In that moment he "dropped to his knees and let out an anguished howl that echoed through the cordillera."[6] In that moment he felt hope slip away, and with that the will to continue. He was sure that they would be rescued, and when that hope died, his sense of purpose and determination died with it. He was a broken man who eventually became yet another victim of the harsh and hostile environment of the Andes.

## A SEARCH FOR HOPE

The story of Job is also a story of the struggle for hope in the midst of human anguish. Everything around Job had given way. His suffering encompassed body, soul, and spirit. He had lost his children and all his earthly belongings. He had lost his health and was engulfed in oozing sores from head to feet. He lost his reputation, the high opinion and respect of those around him—including his wife, who saw him as a fool for not cursing God. But he also lost his comfortable and neat understanding of God: If you were good, God blessed, and if you weren't, God cursed.

As Job's "comforters" gave him their easy answers to his dilemma, Job struggled to find hope in spite of their words. Human hope seemed gone. He longed for the grave as his only hope of relief. He longed for someone to arbitrate between him and God as hope for his justification. But these hopes were elusive and so he said of God, "He uproots my hope like a tree" (Job 19:10).

What a picture! A tree that is uprooted is yanked from its place; it's pulled up from all that gave it support and nourishment. Job's hope had been yanked up from all that gave it substance and life.

Then Job found solid footing again. He looked beyond himself and his present suffering and found hope—solid, unwavering hope as he declared:

*"I know that my Redeemer lives,*
  *and that in the end he will stand upon the earth.*

*And after my skin has been destroyed,*
  *yet in my flesh I will see God;*
*I myself will see him with my own eyes—*
  *I, and not another.*
*How my heart yearns within me!" (19:25–27)*

Wow! What a contrast to the rest of Job's remarks. He had found a hope that could not be uprooted by any amount of human suffering, and he longed for the fulfillment of that hope. I love how Job prefaces these words:

*"Oh, that my words were recorded,*
  *that they were written on a scroll,*
*that they were inscribed with an iron tool on lead,*
  *or engraved in rock forever!" (19:23–24)*

Job could never have imagined that his words would be engraved by God in Holy Scripture to be read and sung and declared for centuries to come, and to offer hope to many in their times of suffering.

### THE HEALING POWER OF HOPE

My friend Kathy has been a modern-day example of this kind of hope. In chapter 7 I wrote about the disappearance of Kathy's parents. As human hope diminished in the days following their disappearance, Job's hope found its place in Kathy's heart and took root there. As others talked about "worst-case scenario," Kathy rested in the reality that her parents knew the same Redeemer who gave hope to Job and that the worst-case scenario humanly would result in the best-case scenario for her parents. And it did.

Weeks later, when their bodies were found, Kathy took great comfort in the reality that those remains were truly that. They were what remained of the earthly part of her parents, while the eternal part was safe with the Lord they loved so much.

Her mother, in her confused and angry state, had wanted to take them "home." God, in His mercy, answered the yearning of her heart and brought them both home, where they are free from the ravages of Alzheimer's disease and from the heartaches, confusion, and frustration of this life. They are home and safe—eternally safe.

Never underestimate the healing power of hope. Years ago I counseled a young woman named Rachel (not her real name) who had suffered abuse from a family member when she was a child. She despised herself and often assumed that everyone else did too. She felt ugly and worthless and, as is often the case, had married a man who did nothing to alleviate those feelings. But the most crippling aftermath of her abuse was her belief that she would always be like this—that the shame and horror of what had happened to her was the shroud she would wear the rest of her life. She saw no hope.

How could I reach into the despair and pain of this woman's heart with God's healing love? As I prayed and sought His wisdom, His instructions became clear: Offer her hope. I realized the importance of replacing the lies of the Enemy with God's truth—the truth that has the power to set us free (John 8:32). And I needed to begin with the truth that there was hope.

What an amazing impact hope had on Rachel's life. It freed her to conquer, one by one, all the other lies that had held her in their grip for so many years. And today she is a vibrant testimony to the power of hope as the first step to emotional healing.

## DON'T LOSE HEART

In 2 Corinthians 4:16–18 we find powerful words that give us a basis for legitimate hope:

> Therefore we do not lose heart. Though outwardly we are wasting away, yet inwardly we are being renewed day by day. For our light and momentary troubles are achieving for us an eternal glory that far outweighs them all. So we fix our eyes not on what is seen, but on what is unseen. For what is seen is temporary, but what is unseen is eternal.

These verses begin with an encouragement: "Therefore we do not lose heart." In other words, we don't lose hope. In *The Amplified Version* this passage paints a dramatic picture of what it is to lose hope: "Therefore we do not become discouraged (utterly spiritless, exhausted, and wearied out through fear)." Why? Because there is a real, solid basis for our hope, as Paul describes in the next verses.

Paul begins by giving us a glimpse into what is going on outwardly. He says, "Outwardly we are wasting away." Not an encouraging picture, and certainly not a basis for hope. But that is only a part the picture. The rest is found in the reality of what is going on inwardly. "Inwardly, we are being renewed day by day."

I saw such a vivid example of this when I visited a woman I had not seen in many years. Julia Derr, who had been a wonderful role model to me when I was a teenager, was now in a nursing home. She had spent years in India as a missionary, but when I first knew her she was retired, which only meant she wasn't in India. She continued to seek out her beloved Indian people wherever she could here in this country and reach out to them with God's eternal message of love.

Now Julia was "wasting away outwardly," and I had been warned that she would probably not know me or be able to respond to me. As I approached her room, I saw her sitting slumped over in a wheelchair with drool coming down one side of her mouth. My immediate and inappropriate reaction was, "God, this isn't fair!" But I only saw the outward Julia. God, in His great kindness, blessed me with a peek into the inward Julia.

As I entered the room, she glanced up with a wonderful look of recognition and joy. She reached up and pulled me down close to her and then, as if she could read my thoughts, said, "Esther, God is still so good and I love Him so much."

God let me see the part of Julia that was being renewed by His wonderful Spirit day by day. It was a beautiful demonstration of hope—one that I will never forget.

## HOPE'S GREATEST ENEMY

Hope may be difficult to define and it may be hard to measure its impact in our lives, but its importance is fully understood by the Enemy of our souls. When Dante wrote of the Inferno in *The Divine Comedy*, he envisioned these words over the gates of Hell: "All hope abandon ye who enter here." He understood that the warden of that eternal prison continually tries to rob us of the hope that is rightfully ours as children of God. He can't touch our eternal hope, but he wants to bring us to our knees in anguish and despair. He wants us to experience that same sense of utter hopelessness that brought Marcelo to his knees high in the Andes, that same hopelessness that haunted those prisoners as the heavy doors of Angola prison slammed and locked behind them.

Satan is no gentleman. He will not back off when times are rough. He doesn't sympathetically step aside when he sees us suffering. He watches for our moments of vulnerability and attacks, and his arrows are aimed straight for our hope. To wound us there is to strike a debilitating blow.

Amy Carmichael expresses it like this: "We know the great part that hope is meant to play in life by the unwearied persistence of the attack upon it. . . . the great enemy of souls tries to undermine or overturn our hope; and when hope goes, joy and peace go with it. In this way he scores a triple victory and we are indeed laid low."[7]

A tool that the Enemy often uses is our own imagination. Hope is an emotional investment in our future. It is believing that in the end there will be relief or a solution—something that will be better than what we are presently experiencing. When we allow our imaginations to project our worst fears into the future, we lose that hope. When Satan paints a picture of what's ahead during our times of suffering, he never adds the brushstrokes of grace or peace. He never adds the presence of the Almighty into the picture. His work is a fake!

What a sharp contrast to God's words of hope and assurance to us found in the familiar words of Jeremiah 29:11: "'For I know the plans I have for you,' declares the LORD, 'plans to prosper you and not to harm you, plans to give you hope and a future.'" That's the picture that God offers us of our future—a picture that has hope as its background. What a beautiful picture done for us by the Master Artist himself, and all of His artwork is genuine and based on His unfailing love and the faithfulness of His word.

Isaiah 26:3 encourages us with the reminder that God will keep us in perfect peace when our mind is stayed or focused on Him. *Young's Literal Translation of the Holy Bible* uses the word "imagination" instead of "mind": "You will keep him in perfect peace whose *imagination* is stayed on You." What depth of meaning that offers to that same verse. Our imagination, which projects images of the future, is going to *stay focused* on thoughts of Christ. That brings hope into all of our thoughts about our uncertain future.

Someday hope will be fulfilled. Heaven is our ultimate hope and will bring a triumphant, victorious end to all of our suffering. But in the meantime, we can know the transforming power of hope now! We find that what can't be easily defined can be wonderfully experienced as we choose to believe the God of hope.

If Dante imagined that hell demanded that all hope be abandoned, imagine the sign that could be over the entrance into heaven: "Claim hope's fulfillment, you who enter!"

Suffering will be no more, but the sweetness will remain forever!

# Notes

## Introduction

1.  Max Lucado, *In the Eye of the Storm* (Dallas: Word Publishing, 1994), 63.
2.  Amy Carmichael, *Gold by Moonlight* (London: Society for Promoting Christian Knowledge, 1940).

## Chapter 1: The Sweetness of His Voice

1.  Peter Lord, *Keeping the Doors Open* (Tarrytown, NY: Chosen Books, 1992).
2.  Charles Austin Miles, "In the Garden."

## Chapter 2: The Sweetness of Knowing God

1.  Charles Haddon Spurgeon, *The Power of Prayer in a Believer's Life* (Lynnwood, WA: Emerald Books, 1993), 47.
2.  Lucado, *In the Eye of the Storm*, 63.
3.  George MacDonald, *Your Life in Christ*, ed., Michael Phillips (Minneapolis: Bethany House, 2005), 111.
4.  J. Hudson Taylor, *A Retrospect* (Chicago: Moody Press, n.d.), 101.

## Chapter 3: The Sweetness of His Care

1.  V. Raymond Edman, *They Found the Secret* (Grand Rapids: Zondervan, 1960), 114.

## Chapter 4: The Sweetness of Surrender

1. Andrew Murray, *Waiting on God* (Chicago: Moody Press, n.d.), 73.
2. Hannah Whitall Smith, *The Christian's Secret of a Happy Life* (Westwood, NJ: Fleming H. Revell), 150.
3. Ibid., 151.
4. Ibid., 143.
5. William Backus, *Hidden Rift with God* (Minneapolis: Bethany House Publishers, 1990).

## Chapter 5: The Sweetness of Shared Suffering

1. Nando Parrado with Vince Rause, *Miracle in the Andes* (New York: Crown Publishing, 2006), 278.

## Chapter 6: The Sweetness of His Comfort

1. Amy Carmichael, *Thou Givest—They Gather* (Fort Washington, PA: CLC, Inc.,1958), 72
2. Melody Green, *No Compromise: The Life Story of Keith Green* (Chatsworth, CA: Sparrow Press, 1989), 277.
3. Ibid.

## Chapter 8: The Sweetness of His Grace

1. Jim Cymbala, *Fresh Power* (Grand Rapids: Zondervan, 2001), 156.
2. Corrie ten Boom, *The Hiding Place* (Grand Rapids: Chosen Books, 1971), 215.
3. *The Oswald Chambers Devotional Reader,* ed., Harry Verploegh (Nashville: Thomas Nelson, 1990), 106.

## Chapter 9: The Sweetness of His Correction

1. Amy Carmichael, *Gold Chord* (Fort Washington, PA: Christian Literature Crusade, 1957), 69–70.
2. Andrew Murray, *The Path to Holiness* (Minneapolis: Bethany House, 1984), 202.

## Chapter 10: The Sweetness of Hope

1. *The Tozer Topical Reader, Vol. 1,* Comp. Ron Eggert (Camp Hill, PA: Christian Publications, Inc., 1998), 275.
2. Jerome Groopman, MD, *The Anatomy of Hope* (New York: Random House, 2004), 212.
3. Ibid., xiv.
4. Nando Parrado with Vince Rause, *Miracle in the Andes* (New York: Crown Publishing, 2006), 63.
5. Ibid., 63.
6. Ibid., 104.
7. Amy Carmichael, *Whispers of His Power* (Old Tappan, NJ: Fleming H. Revell, 1982), 36.

# Scripture Index

## OLD TESTAMENT

## New Testament

# About the Author

## M. ESTHER LOVEJOY

ESTHER WAS PRIVILEGED to serve the Lord in full-time ministry for over twenty-five years. She has enjoyed ministering to women as a Bible teacher and as a retreat and conference speaker. Presently she has a radio ministry, *View from the Sparrow's Nest*, and an Internet blog of the same name (viewfromthesparrowsnest.com). She is a contributing author to *Inspired by Tozer*, a recent publication by Regal Books.

Esther lives in Leland, North Carolina, with her husband, Peter. They are empty-nesters, with the exception of Peter's mother who is ninety-four. Peter and Esther share nine children and twenty of the cutest and smartest grandchildren.

# Note to the Reader

THE PUBLISHER INVITES you to share your response to the message of this book by writing Discovery House Publishers, P.O. Box 3566, Grand Rapids, MI 49501, U.S.A. For information about other Discovery House books, music, videos, or DVDs, contact us at the same address or call 1-800-653-8333. Find us on the Internet at www.dhp.org or send e-mail to books@dhp.org.